Voices of Advent

Voices of Advent
The Bible's Insights for a Season of Hope

Voices of Advent
978-1-7910-3631-7
978-1-7910-3632-4 eBook

Voices of Advent: DVD
978-1-7910-3635-5

Voices of Advent: Leader Guide
978-1-7910-3633-1
978-1-7910-3634-8 eBook

MATTHEW L. SKINNER

VOICES
OF ADVENT

THE BIBLE'S INSIGHTS FOR A SEASON OF HOPE

ABINGDON PRESS | NASHVILLE

Voices of Advent

The Bible's Insights for a Season of Hope

Library of Congress Control Number: 2025937584
978-1-7910-3631-7

Cover description for *Voices of Advent: The Bible's Insights for a Season of Hope* by Matthew L. Skinner. A snowy forest under a night sky with northern lights appears above a blue and gold band featuring the title and subtitle. The author's name is in gold at the bottom over a starry, blue-toned background.

MANUFACTURED IN THE UNITED STATES OF AMERICA

To Karoline

Here's to new beginnings

CONTENTS

PREFACE

Although advertisers tell us "the Christmas season" begins right after Thanksgiving in the United States—even in early November, if you believe the playlist of a radio station where I live—Christians have traditionally followed a different timeline. Advent, the four weeks prior to Christmas, exists as a separate season, one of expectant preparation and hope. When the season concludes and ushers us into celebrating the birth of Jesus, we have had four weeks to take stock of how much we need Jesus in the first place.

Various voices from the Bible speak to us in the prayers, songs, readings, and sermons that fill the Advent season. Many of those voices prepare us to welcome a newborn king who will transform our world. Some of the voices are more cosmic in scope, dwelling on wonder and majesty. Others of them have a decidedly nitty-gritty and occasionally disconcerting message. Yet all of them ready us to encounter Jesus in their own ways.

This book guides us into Advent hope in four parts, paying attention to biblical voices and pointing a way toward a deeper appreciation of the season. Advent involves more than taking a trek to Bethlehem and ratcheting up our excitement. The book's purpose is to explore biblical texts to consider how they lead us to reflect on God, live our lives, express faith, set our priorities, and celebrate Christmas at the end of Advent. Over four chapters, we will listen to Jesus as he promises to reveal himself again in the future and complete his work on the world's behalf, to John the Baptist as he prepares the way for the Messiah who transforms the world, to faithful and visionary people who poetically anticipate the magnificence of Jesus's birth as God's greatest gift to us, and to angels and visionaries who praise God when Christmas finally dawns. Listen carefully to the voices, and you'll hear hope in all of them. Advent, then, is more than the *beginning* of "the church year" or "the Christmas season"; it's the *overture* that sets the tone for everything that follows in the story about Jesus, all the way to its end. Like any good overture, it introduces themes that will come back to us later, because it knows where the overall story is headed. Advent orients us to a sense of ultimate purpose—God's and ours.

The Bible never instructs Christians how to celebrate Advent. In fact, Scripture isn't interested in dictating how most of our religious rituals should be structured. The apostle Paul's teaching about how *not* to celebrate the Lord's Supper in 1 Corinthians 11:17-34 is the most prominent exception. My aim isn't to make or enforce a plan that you must follow in Advent. In this book I'll present a number of passages and themes from the Gospels that guide us into a variety of ways that we can expect Jesus to *arrive* among us. By exploring those expectations, we increase our understanding of what it means to hope in Jesus Christ—both for the present and for the future we desire.

I'm a Bible scholar who teaches at a Christian seminary, so this book will offer guidance about Scripture and how we let its numerous voices express themselves in their own particular accents, coming to us from thousands of years ago from very different cultural environments. I've written this book to be accessible to a wide range of people, no matter how familiar you might or might not already be with the Bible and the ancient settings in which it was written. Obviously there are other voices beyond the Bible that shape our approaches to Advent, especially in familiar music and symbolism, and I'll mention some of those along the way too.

Here at the outset I should probably confess that I love to celebrate Advent. It is my favorite season for worshipping, for pondering the mysteries of faith, and for orienting my life as best I can in response to God's love and goodness. I find Advent simultaneously reassuring and disruptive in my own heart. I experience hope in the gentle solace of a hymn like "Comfort, Comfort Now My People." At the same time, I feel called to put my hope into action and to break out of my spiritual doldrums when we sing the "Canticle of the Turning (My Soul Cries Out with a Joyful Shout)," with its reminders that God has promised to upend the world and set it to rights. I need hope to survive, and Advent comes to me as a season designed to stir up hope. That's because Advent, as we will see, keeps us focused on Jesus's commitment to be with us, to arrive into our circumstances again and again.

I hope this book generates a similar response in you, that is, a greater sense of both Advent relief and Advent restlessness. Along the way, you'll learn more about the Bible and find opportunities to reflect on its capacity to stretch our imagination about what's true and what's possible. More than that, I hope you learn more about yourself and about God. May this investigation of the voices of Advent leave you appreciating the ways that faith expresses itself through our efforts to wait actively on God. May Advent cultivate in you a visceral, urgent longing—one that grows out of a desire to see the goodness that God has promised finally bloom in full flower.

INTRODUCTION

WAITING IN HOPE FOR THE MESSIAH'S ARRIVALS

In churches we use a lot of words whose meanings are easy to forget. We've become accustomed to using certain terms without thinking about them, almost like jargon. Words like *gospel, baptism,* and *Eucharist,* for example, didn't arise in the church; they weren't coined to be uniquely Christian words. *Gospel* means, simply, "good news." We inherited baptism and Eucharist from ancient Greek vocabulary for "dipping" and "thanksgiving."

The names of the church's seasons probably belong on the list of those words. Advent, Epiphany, and Lent might all sound very "churchy" to you. But Lent refers to the lengthening of daylight hours during the weeks before Easter (at least in the Northern Hemisphere!). Epiphany means "manifestation" or "realization," referring to how Jesus's true identity becomes perceptible in Gospel stories such as the visit of the magi (or the "three kings" in some traditions), Jesus's baptism, and the Transfiguration.

Advent, which English borrows from the Latin word *adventus,* means "arrival" or "coming." During Advent, we anticipate the arrival of Jesus. As we will soon discuss, however, that means more than just getting ready to celebrate Christmas. Jesus arrives more than once.

Advent is a season of waiting and also preparing. That's what we do when we anticipate someone's arrival. Sometimes we wait for events or people that may not ever finally get here. I moved to Minnesota over twenty-three years ago, and I've met many born-and-bred Minnesotans who talk about waiting for the Vikings to win a Super Bowl, but they speak as if they suspect it will never happen. It's only wishful thinking for them. (To be fair, some of them are simply convinced that they have been cursed by the universe.) But it's a different experience to wait for something that we know is definitely coming. Maybe you have an upcoming vacation planned and purchased, or a friend has invited you to dinner next Thursday. That's the kind of anticipation that swirls in the Advent air. We wait and prepare for what we know is coming. A confidence propels us forward. We walk through Advent, then, in hope.

IT'S NOT JUST ABOUT CHRISTMAS

What are we hoping for? Really, Advent is about a *who*, not a *what*. We anticipate the coming of God's Messiah, the Christ. (Let me return us to thinking about the meaning of our common religious terms. Both *Messiah* and *Christ* mean "Anointed One." Messiah comes into English from Hebrew. Christ comes from Greek. The words are synonyms in English, referring to the One whom God has designated, or "anointed," to carry out God's ultimate purposes. For Christians, of course this is Jesus. We've become so used to this language, however, that it's as if we assume Christ is just Jesus's last name.)

In Advent we recognize that it's a complicated thing to talk about "anticipating Jesus." Wasn't Jesus of Nazareth born two thousand years ago but is no longer physically among us? *Yes.* Don't we talk about Jesus being present with us now, and doesn't Jesus say in the Bible that he will be with us always, until the end (Matthew 28:20)? *Yes.* Hasn't the Christian church always taught that God isn't finished with the world and that Jesus will return in the future to bring all things to completion? *Yes. Good questions!* (I used to teach Sunday school for junior high-schoolers. They kept me on my toes and sometimes shaking in fear. I'm familiar with being interrogated with religious questions like this.) I'm saying: Most of us know that all of those questions are answered "*Yes.*" As Christians we are always anticipating Jesus in numerous ways. He has led us to count on him, promising that he will keep showing up in a variety of means.

Advent, standing as it does at the beginning of the church's calendar, tells us to expect multiple dimensions of Jesus's arrival. The season starts the new year for Christians by saying, "Get ready to welcome him—not just at Christmas but all year long."

I'm pretty sure that putting, "Get ready to meet your God!" on a sign in front of your church is not an effective or loving way to preach the good news to your neighbors, but it isn't a bad summary of what Advent is about. Get ready! One of the things I love most about Advent—its traditions, its hymns, its symbolism—is how it asks us to anticipate Jesus Christ not with fear but with seriousness mixed with awe. It's a season of humility and joy. Those postures we assume during Advent fuel our hope in God and in what God may yet do.

Some Roman Catholic teachers have characterized Advent as a season in which we prepare to encounter Jesus Christ in history, mystery, and majesty. In other words, Advent is a season with an ability to move us around through time, so we can view Jesus and all he means for us from a variety of perspectives—past, present, and future. Advent provides a way of anticipating the big picture of what God *set in motion* when a young woman from an out-of-the-way village gave birth to Jesus in Bethlehem. In Advent, then, we remember the Messiah's birth (in *history*). We expect Jesus to come to us again each and every Christmas in our present-day experience (in *mystery*). We pine for his eventual return to us (in *majesty*), so God might finally make "all things new" (Revelation 21:5).

Listen to the hymns of Advent. Light a candle on a wreath. Organize a drive to collect goods to help supply a local food shelf. Themes of promise and fulfillment make up the soundtrack of the season. We reflect on how far the world and ourselves are from fulfilling God's intentions, and we celebrate God's faithfulness, because God has pledged to redeem us and the whole creation. As I said, we reflect on that with a willingness to move around through time. Advent points us forward as we ponder the ultimate promises God has yet to fulfill. Advent calls us back into the past as we relive the promises God has already kept in sending Jesus, the child born to Mary and Joseph. Through it all, we open our hearts to Christ among us, praying that Jesus might, as the Christmas carol "O Little Town of Bethlehem" puts it, once again "be born in us today."[1]

A Very Short History of Advent

Easter was the original Big Holy Day for churches. It was not until the fourth century of the Common Era that Christians widely began to observe Christmas. Eventually the holiday (or "holy day") grew into the church's second major annual feast day. Feasts usually need to be preceded by an extended period of fasting, however. For one reason, it takes work to prepare a feast and moderation to save the food you need for a supersized party. That was especially true for people in medieval Europe, because food was relatively scarce in December. Another reason is less practical and more spiritual: Abstaining from food—either entirely or in moderation—is considered by many an exercise in religious devotion meant to deepen a person's sense of reliance on God alone. Fasting was not viewed as punishment but as something that can benefit your spiritual vitality and help you prepare for all that Christmas declares about God's reliability and generosity.

Moving into the fifth and sixth centuries, people in some regions fasted for three weeks prior to Christmas, while in other places it was six weeks or forty days. Some regularity began to emerge when Pope Gregory I (Gregory the Great, 590–604) decreed it should be a four-week fast, which remains the length of Advent today (the four Sundays before Christmas). The season of Advent, then, began as an extended fast. Easter was already in place in the spring, with Lent as its preceding fast. In the way that Advent and Christmas became ritualized, they provided a kind of complement to Lent and Easter.

Lent focuses largely on penitence in many Christian traditions. Advent, on the other hand, typically focuses on waiting and preparation—not necessarily trimming a tree and baking cookies but orienting our spiritual lives and shaping our consciences.

Some of what I mentioned earlier, preparing for the Messiah to arrive in a number of different ways and at various points in time, was baked into Advent early in this history. Christian authors as far back as Justin Martyr (from the second century, long before Christians considered Christmas a holiday worth celebrating) saw a connection between Jesus's birth and his promised return. Justin wrote, concerning Jesus:

> The prophets have proclaimed before two comings [or "arrivals"] of his: one, which has already happened, as that of a dishonored and suffering man; and the second, when, as has been proclaimed, he will come from heaven with glory with his angelic host; when also he will raise the bodies of all the people who have lived.[2]

My point is simply that for a long time Christians have drawn a connection between the birth of Jesus and his ultimate, future return. Those two events are, in a sense, bookends of his work as Savior. Both events are world-altering. As a result, Christians have seen the connection as deserving our attention and emphasis as we begin each new year of worshipping God and laboring together on God's behalf.

I'll have more to say about Jesus's future return and the significance of Advent (both the word *Advent* and the season) in chapter 1.

Don't misunderstand this brief review of the origins of Advent as my attempt to claim that there is only one right or authorized way to celebrate the season. But it is important for us to recognize, I think, that our Christian ancestors through the centuries have found value in treating the season as more than a countdown to December 25. Advent provides an overture to the entire Christian experience. By turning our attention to Jesus's presence—past, present, and future— Advent infuses in us Christ-centered perspectives about God's commitment to the world and about the meaning of our lives.

Different congregations commemorate Advent in different ways, but there has been a general pattern of Advent observance in Western (Protestant and Roman Catholic) churches in recent centuries:

- First Sunday: Preparing for Jesus Christ's future, consummating arrival (or return).
- Second and third Sundays: Heeding John the Baptist's exhortations and promises about the coming of the Messiah over two thousand years ago.
- Fourth Sunday: Listening in on God's communications to Mary and Joseph and observing how they respond to the extraordinary news about what they are experiencing as they prepare for Jesus's birth.

Those themes dwell in the biblical passages—at least, the ones taken from the Gospels—that are frequently chosen to be read in worship during Advent. Preachers often take their cues from those passages as they guide congregations through the season.

What I appreciate about the pattern is that it begins with emotions of yearning and restlessness. Advent starts by asking us to acknowledge something true: We certainly do not live in the best of all possible worlds, and we long for God to heal the problems, injustices, and griefs that we cannot fix. Those are feelings as valid now as they have been in any century. We remind ourselves that there are still promises that God has yet to keep about securing the well-being of humanity and the whole creation. We imagine a new future as we make our way through an often difficult present.

Next, after that first Sunday, we recognize that God has already started turning the wheels of fulfillment; God has already proved to be reliable. The first Christmas in Bethlehem gives evidence of that. John the Baptist's huge expectations about the Messiah remind us that the birth and ministry of Jesus stand as a kind of pledge or down payment that reaffirms God's commitment to transform the world.

Then, as Christmas draws close, we witness the amazement that arises when God comes near to us and the world. We examine Mary's and Joseph's experiences, not to breathe an aroma of nostalgia, but to explore the wonder of what it is like to have Christ arrive among us—extremely up close. What is our response? How do we participate? How do we describe what is going on at Christmas? What will it mean for us, for our neighbors, and for our world?

Once again, then, we see elements of past, present, and future entwined during Advent. As adorable as it is to see baby Jesus in a manger at Christmas, Advent has always provided a reminder that he refuses to stay put there. Jesus won't stay relegated only to history.

The Messiah also has some present-day mystery and future majesty to attend to.

How to Wait

Whoever first had the idea of making Advent calendars with a piece of chocolate hidden behind each door, one for each day, might have been a cruel person who liked making children suffer. At least, that's what I used to think. When I was young, I failed to understand why someone could give me two dozen candies as a gift, yet I was expected to obey some kind of unstated consumption agreement that stipulated I could eat only one each day. This was supposed to build character or patience in me? (Then again, maybe it worked. I'm pretty disciplined now with Advent calendars, since growing older has convinced me I should limit myself to one chocolate per day. However, I do eat my daily piece of chocolate from the calendar first thing in the morning. Because it's mine. Obviously I wouldn't have done well with Advent fasting if I had lived in medieval Europe.) What I'm getting at is this: I don't believe it's true that somehow each delicious sweet will be more satisfying if you have to wait for it or prove you have enough self-control to deserve it.

Advent is a season of waiting, but it's not a season of pointless waiting. I want to be very clear about that. We're only halfway through the introduction, but I don't want you to give up on the book already because you might be worrying that I'm going to describe Advent as an exercise in learning the benefits of delayed gratification. I won't. I'm not like the dad in the old Calvin and Hobbes comic strips who was always pontificating on the activities that would "build character" for poor Calvin.

It's true that when we take Advent seriously we might hold off on singing "Joy to the World" until we've worked our way through more mellow tunes such as "In the Bleak Midwinter" or "My Soul in Stillness Waits." That's not saying we have to ration joy or dial down the fervor of our hope. The waiting we do in Advent isn't about a willingness to endure discomfort or a commitment to strengthening our capacity for patience. Pondering Advent does not mean adjusting your expectations to match God's timetable without complaint. In Advent we extol the importance of active, even insistent, waiting. I hear a low grumble in the things that Christians and the Bible say about God during Advent. The church grows fidgety, expecting something to happen. We're asking God to show up. Actually, we're imploring God. We stand on the cusp of where waiting is about to turn into action.

The active waiting I'm talking about begins with taking stock and doing some honest evaluation. I don't know about you, but I'm really good at taking stock of other people's shortcomings. It's much easier and more pleasant than owning up to my own. That's likely why a lot of the voices we hear from the Bible during Advent call us to look inside ourselves and do some self-inspection.

In the chapters to come, we'll explore some of the ways in which biblical passages can encourage us to do that kind of internal housecleaning. For now, however, consider the first verse of the Advent hymn "O Lord, How Shall I Meet You":

> O Lord, how shall I meet you,
> how welcome you aright?
> Your people long to greet you,
> my hope, my heart's delight!
> O kindle, Lord most holy,

> a lamp within my breast,
> to do in spirit lowly
> all that may please you best.[3]

Notice that the hymn characterizes the church as people who *long* to greet God. (That could be risky, as we will discuss shortly!) It recognizes the need to do so properly ("aright"). It asks God to cultivate in us humility and a desire to act as God would have us act, presumably following the pattern of Jesus Christ. It dwells on the importance of examining ourselves and declares that we, Jesus's people, "long to greet" him. By the way, the second and third verses of this hymn, if you want to find them on the internet, speak about the love God shows in becoming human in the birth of Jesus and about Jesus returning one day in glory "to bring an end to sadness and bid our fears be still." Once again: Past, present, and future converge in an Advent reflection, directing us to encounter Jesus in history, mystery, and majesty.

This call to introspection is not the same thing as the church trying to be a moral scold or aiming to make people feel bad about themselves. It's about raising the stakes. Remember, the foundational conviction that gives shape to Advent is that we are getting ready to meet God—here, among us. There will be surprises along the way in how God comes to us, but the fact remains that this is serious business. Things change when God shows up.

Let me illustrate what I mean by "serious business." Not long after I started teaching at my seminary, a colleague on the faculty introduced me to a short sermon originally preached on the first Sunday of Advent in 1928 by Dietrich Bonhoeffer, a German pastor who was executed by the Nazis in 1945 due to his association with a group that was plotting to assassinate Hitler.[4] Several sentences from the sermon have become unforgettable to me. I routinely refer to them when I teach about the Gospels. Bonhoeffer marvels at the fact that Christians often talk rather casually about meeting Jesus or walking with Jesus:

> We have become so accustomed to the idea of divine love and of God's coming at Christmas that we no longer feel the shiver of fear that God's coming should arouse in us. We are indifferent to the message, taking only the pleasant and agreeable out of it and forgetting the serious aspect, that the God of the world draws near to the people of our little earth and lays claim to us. The coming of God is truly not only glad tidings, but first of all frightening news for everyone who has a conscience.

In other words, centuries of reflection on Christmas as an eruption of magnificent love have dulled our sense of "the fear of the Lord" that the Bible often mentions. If you need an example, consult the story of Moses encountering God on Mount Sinai, a scene full of all kinds of signs and sounds of the divine presence, while everyone else at the base of the mountain quakes in terror (Exodus 20:18-21).

Rest assured, Bonhoeffer was trying neither to take all the joy out of Christmas nor to make everyone feel too worthless to encounter Jesus. He wanted his listeners to slow down for a minute and contemplate the majesty of what we celebrate at Christmas. He wanted to impress upon them the utter surprise they should experience in the face of God's *vulnerability* as one who becomes human like you and I are.

Our reflections in Advent should not leave us paralyzed in fear or convinced that God is too good to be associated with us. Bonhoeffer explains the purpose of our Advent introspections in the sermon's next sentences:

> Only when we have felt the terror of the matter, can we recognize the incomparable kindness. God comes into the very midst of evil and of death, and judges the evil in us and in the world. And by judging us, God cleanses and sanctifies us, comes to us with grace and love. God makes us happy as only children can be happy. God wants to always be with us, wherever we may be—in our sin, in our suffering and death. We are no longer alone; God is with us.

God wants to be with us. God will be with us. Those are massive claims that should cause us to reassess our tremendous value in God's estimation. The second Creation story at the beginning of Genesis describes God being very close to humanity, forming and breathing life into the first human being and then walking in the garden where humanity lives (Genesis 2:7; 3:8). At the other cover of the Bible, in last two chapters of the Book of Revelation, we read statements about God dwelling among humanity in the future (Revelation 21:3, 22-23; 22:3-5).

From start to finish the Bible is full of statements about God's desire to share space and relationship with humanity and the whole creation. If God is willing—actually *eager*—to be among us, anything's possible. Advent tells a very large story.

Because an expectation of—and a longing for—God's nearness lends so much energy to the voices that speak during Advent, the kind of waiting we do during this season is anything but passive or dormant. The active waiting I mentioned earlier begins with self-examination, but it also entails a hunger to see things change and a willingness to get involved.

During Advent we admit that the world could be better. We expect that God has better things in mind for us, for our neighbors, for those who are neglected, for future generations, and for our planet. We pray for change. There is a hint of protest in our Advent practices, prayers, and pronouncements. If you know any of the verses to the Advent hymn "O Come, O Come, Emmanuel," you get the idea. They beg God to repair the problems that harm humanity. They issue imperatives. Set people free! Bless people with your knowledge and guidance! Save us! Pour out your comfort! End the divisions among humankind! Establish peace! And then there's the repetition of "O come!": Come on God, get moving! We're ready for you to unleash every ounce of the goodness you've promised. We're tired of all the suffering.

In the chapters of this book, when we start digging into biblical passages, we'll see more of this dissatisfaction with the way things are, but we will also notice an expectation that God will indeed act. The voices that speak from Scripture during Advent never give way to cynicism or disillusionment. Stirred up by hope, they instill hope. And hope produces courage.

That's why Advent hope is active hope and not a hope that is content to sit on the sidelines with its arms crossed while watching to see if anything will ever get better. Remember, Christian hope is more about confident expectation than it is about optimism or wishful thinking, because hope is a product of the trustworthiness that God has already demonstrated to us.

With that kind of hope in our hearts, it's hard to remain disengaged, as if we have nothing to contribute but our thoughts and prayers for God's desired future to come to pass. In the biblical passages we'll explore, we'll discover a lot of talk about God—who God is, what God does, and what God will do. This "talk about God" matters for us too. The voices of Advent utter invitations for us to stay close, to play a part, and to make ourselves available to God.

Introduction

In some of the biblical scenes we'll explore, it will look like everything is falling apart and the world is straining under the weight of its own chaos, but we will also read that those times are vital opportunities for the church to preach and live out the gospel in a social landscape that looks hopeless. In other passages there will be warnings about not being ready for the Messiah. Some of those parts of the Bible speak about times when doubts seem able to overwhelm faith, but we also find reassuring stories of people willing to put their own well-being on the line for the sake of participating in what God intends. Still other biblical passages describe the coming of Jesus as something that fits within a mammoth, cosmic scope. Yet even within that immensity we read about our value to God. Finally, there will be stories of courage and care, reminding us that the birth of Jesus obligates us to seek the welfare of others. We have parts to play.

VOICES FROM THE BIBLE

As I said earlier, there is no single correct or authorized way to celebrate Advent. I want to be transparent, nevertheless, about why I have organized this book as I have.

First, the book's main focus is on Scripture. I've talked a lot in this introduction about Advent in general, its history, and some of its hymns. I'm setting us up for the main course, which is to discover that our engagement with the Bible itself might generate insights for enriching our spiritual lives and our experiences of Advent and Christmas. I'm asking you to join me in observing that the Bible places a high premium on preparing ourselves and keeping our expectations high. Those are useful responses for us if we want to foster a hope-filled Advent.

Second, we will direct almost all of our attention to just one section of Christian Scripture: the four Gospels. This would have to be a much longer book if I were to give the Old Testament and the Epistles the time they deserve. Even though I am limiting our exploration to the Gospels, please do not conclude that the rest of the Bible is not helpful during Advent or not relevant to discussions of Christian hope. I can hardly imagine an Advent without the visions of Isaiah or the poetry of the Psalms. George Frideric Handel and his librettist Charles Jennens were on to something when they created *The Messiah* almost entirely from quotations from the Old Testament, the Epistles, and the Book of Revelation.

Third, while I was guided by the four-week progression I described above as I reviewed the history of Advent, I do not follow it exactly. I want to spend extended time with Luke's and John's elevated poetry about the advent of Jesus of Nazareth. I also recognize the value in investigating the birth narratives in Matthew and Luke, for they help us see that hope does not dissipate when the Bible's stories move from expecting Jesus to welcoming him.

Finally, let me move us out of this introduction and start to transport us back in time, into the testimony of Scripture, with some comments on the distance between ancient cultural contexts and the circumstances of most people whom I expect will read this book.

If, as you read on, it seems to you that some of the themes at the heart of Advent arise out of experiences of fragility, risk, suffering, and dissatisfaction, you're on to something. The topics we will discuss come from biblical stories that themselves emerged out of ancient people's real ordeals of powerlessness, oppression, frustration, and peril. In fact, nearly all of the Bible arose from circumstances in which people of faith were trying to shore up hope in the midst of turmoil, encourage one another in times of difficulty and confusion, and lay the groundwork for a future that could bring healing after desolation had ended. The New Testament writings, in particular, were composed by authors who never expected a time when the church would have access to the levers that help launch widespread cultural, economic, and political change. When we look back at ancient Christian communities, they were groups of people vastly outnumbered in their societies and sometimes worried that they would suffer as a result. Christmas is certainly about joy, peace, and the assurance of new life, but those promises came to our spiritual ancestors in situations of struggle. The Bible contains their point of view and also speaks to it.

I don't say all of that to make us feel guilty for any modern advantages we might enjoy, nor am I trying to diminish our need for hope. I only want to point out that it profoundly distorts the Bible if privileged people—and I am very much one of them—don't respect the struggles of the people we meet in Scripture. They are different people who lived different lives than I do. I don't want to equate my struggles with theirs, but neither do I want to pretend that I have nothing in common with them. The things that cause me grief, dismay, or fear do not align with what it meant for them to be vulnerable, poor, ostracized, or otherwise at risk. That's fine, as long as I don't try to diminish their plight in the process of bringing my experiences into conversation with theirs. I will try to avoid doing that in the chapters to come, even as I will make the claim that their stories from long ago have power to fuel hope—active hope—among us still today.

CHAPTER 1

THE VOICE OF JESUS
Beginning at the End

Passages We Will Explore:

- Mark 13:24-37
- Matthew 24:29-44
- Luke 21:25-36

I'm one of those people who likes to set up a Christmas tree and decorations as soon as Advent begins. Candles, wreaths, a crèche, garland—I'm here for all the sights, smells, and sounds. The music matters to me too. Instead of jumping into the grand, loud Christmas songs that I turn to when Christmas gets closer, I prefer to start the season with things like Handel's *Messiah*, *The Nutcracker*, and the quieter pensive carols.

One of my favorite things to listen to when the season arrives is a cantata by Johann Sebastian Bach titled, in German, *Wachet auf, ruft uns die Stimme.* It means, "Wake up, the voice calls to us." I sometimes forget the whole title and remember it simply as *Wachet auf*—Wake up!

Bach based this piece, which people sometimes refer to as "Sleepers Awake," on an existing hymn that itself was based on Matthew 25:1-13. In that passage, Jesus tells his followers a parable about ten bridesmaids who fall asleep when a bridegroom is delayed beyond his expected arrival time. When at last he shows up, the drowsy bridesmaids have to respond quickly to light their lamps and get themselves into the wedding banquet. Not all of them are able, and so Jesus ends the parable with a command: "Keep awake, therefore, for you know neither the day nor the hour."

It's an ominous parable, but Bach's composition sounds joyful to me in parts, gentle and kind in others. Mostly it's full of longing. You might have heard parts of the cantata, especially the fourth movement, which was also arranged as an instrumental piece for a pipe organ. You can find performances of it online, if you're curious.

Being told to "Wake up!" is sometimes disorienting and scary. My mother had to say it to me most mornings when I was in high school, and I never appreciated it. But I like starting Advent with a call to snap out of my sleepiness and pay attention. Something's going to happen, the voice implies, and I need to get focused.

The cantata is traditionally performed during Advent, probably because its main theme involves being ready for Christ's return, which is what the parable of the bridesmaids is about.[1] Bach interprets that expectation in loving, comforting tones, because it means our salvation, in all its fullness, is about to arrive (there's that "advent" word again: *arrival*).

As I mentioned in the introduction, Advent isn't just about reliving the anticipation of Jesus's birth two thousand years ago. Advent also involves reflection on another messianic "arrival"—when Jesus comes in majesty, fulfilling promises he makes in the Gospels about returning a second time. That's why people perform *Wachet auf* during Advent, and it's why sometimes on the first Sunday of Advent you'll hear a reading from the Gospels that sounds like it would be more at home in a disaster film or in a novel about a dystopian, terrifying future than in a church. It can be a shock to the system, especially if you were humming along to "The Little Drummer Boy" on the radio while driving to church. (I like that song, too, because I have wide-ranging musical tastes and because the kid with the little drum brought his best.) Your pastor isn't trying to punish you or toughen you up before you get to Christmas stories about shepherds and angels. The point of exploring passages about Jesus's future return is to notice that Jesus's voice in the Gospels is telling us to expect more from him, to expect completion. Before we gather around the manger in Bethlehem, sometimes it's valuable to begin at the end.

In this chapter, then, we will explore what Jesus has to say about his future and ours. Jesus's voice clarifies our vision for what Christmas points to and what we should expect from living our lives in faithful waiting and wakefulness.

Two Greek Words Worth Knowing

To help us explore the biblical passages I'll soon introduce, I need to set the stage and explain aspects of the culture in which Jesus and, later, the Gospels circulated. Specifically, I will describe ways that some of Jesus's Jewish companions were thinking about God as they attempted to live faithfully, make sense of their experiences as people on the losing end of numerous conflicts over multiple centuries, and keep hope alive for their future. I'll do this by teaching you about two Greek words. You can drop them into casual conversation at the holiday get-togethers you attend next Advent and be the life of the party.

The New Testament books don't all use the same language to refer to Jesus's future return, but a Greek word that commonly indicates it is _parousia_. Just a few of the places where it shows up across the New

Testament are Matthew 24:3; 1 Corinthians 15:23; 1 Thessalonians 4:15; James 5:7-8; and 1 John 2:28. Most English translations of the Bible render the noun *parousia* simply as "coming." It can also mean "arrival" or "appearance." As a result, theologians sometimes speak of "the *Parousia*" with a capital *P* as a shorthand reference to Jesus's future return, whatever they understand that event or promise to mean. Now that we're two thousand years beyond Jesus's lifetime, different Christians have different ways of interpreting the specifics of what hope in "the *Parousia*" could be all about. So far, the verdict is out on who's going to get it right.

If the possible meanings of *parousia* sound familiar to you, you're right. *Parousia* is basically the Greek equivalent of the Latin noun *adventus*, which I mentioned in the introduction. In fact, when the Bible was translated into Latin in the late fourth century CE, the translators used *adventus* for all the appearances of *parousia* in the verses I named above. Both mean "arrival."

It's important to know that *parousia* was not a new word for the original audiences of the New Testament writings. It was a common word in the culture, not something specially invented by or about Jesus. You might use it to describe your excitement about a number of things, such as the arrival of summer or the return of volleyball season. At the same time, among Greek-speakers in the ancient Roman-ruled world, a *parousia* could also indicate the manifestation of a god or, more commonly, a visit from a dignitary, such as a high-ranking official in the government or military. In other words, a *parousia* could refer to a big deal with a lot of noise and maybe a parade, so it was unlikely that one would occur in your city without everyone knowing about it. When the New Testament refers to Jesus's *parousia*, it sometimes imagines quite a spectacle. (Fun fact: When the New Testament talks about Jesus returning, the imagery almost always describes him coming back to be with us here, as opposed to him coming to take us away to somewhere else.)

This idea of a returning or (re)arriving Messiah says something about the magnitude of Jesus's power; he will be more impressive than any human emperor or commander. It also suggests that the borders dividing heaven and earth are not so thick and absolute as people might assume. Someone who ascended into heaven will return. From the perspective of Jews in the ancient world, God resided literally "up there," among angels and other heavenly beings. The Christian belief about God being born as a human being and then returning someday means that the boundaries that keep heaven separated from earth cannot hold. Indeed, three Gospels indicate as much when they describe the Holy Spirit coming to Jesus through a rift created when the sky ("the heavens") becomes "torn apart" (Mark 1:10-11; for a less violent opening, see Matthew 3:16-17; Luke 3:21-22). Multiple aspects of the Gospels make Jesus's ministry resemble an incursion or suggest that a cosmic breakthrough is taking place.

That sense of two planes of existence—heaven and earth—impinging on each other, along with the idea of God intruding into human affairs and history in a decisive way, take us to the second Greek word: *apokalupsis*. You probably see an English word hiding in there; it's a term that English adopted straight from Greek: *apocalypse*. There's a problem, however. For most modern English speakers, an apocalypse has come to mean a large-scale disaster. A film about the Vietnam War and the dehumanizing effects of warfare and colonialism, *Apocalypse Now*, had something to do with that. I belong to a generation whose cultural lexicon includes "nuclear apocalypse" and "zombie apocalypse." When we get an epic winter storm in the

Twin Cities, where I live, people refer to it as a "snowpocalypse." The word's original meaning, however, is less dramatic. It doesn't necessarily imply wreckage or violence. An *apokalupsis* is any kind of a revelation or an uncovering. It means now you can perceive or know something you previously did not.

During the two centuries prior to Jesus's birth and the century after it, some Jewish authors (and, after Jesus, Christian authors) composed books that scholars generally refer to as apocalypses. That's because a theme common to those writings is their claim that they reveal something previously unseen or unknown, privileged information that God has revealed to the author. That information might come from a dream (as in the seventh chapter of the Book of Daniel) or from a tour of heaven given to the author (as in the Book of Revelation, a book whose traditional Greek title is *Apokalupsis*).

Those ancient apocalypses are books brimming with symbolism, some reassuring and some grotesque. A number of them describe earthly or angelic battles and claim to perceive the future. For the most part, they describe people on earth living through dire crises and conflicts that inevitably occur before God will break in to make things right. They characterize God as in command of history as opposed to trying to grab the steering wheel from the backseat. They promise judgment to come, in which the holy and unholy will be identified and divided. They speak about resurrection and an afterlife for human beings. Perhaps most notably, for the purposes of our study of Advent, these apocalypses assert that a different reality is possible— indeed, that a different reality is coming. Sometimes they describe places where reward or punishment happens, but also sometimes they foster hope that a new era will soon break in and displace our current one. The apocalypses have plenty of rough edges and occasionally shocking scenes, but they do insist that a better world will come into existence.[2] They offer reassurances to their audiences, even when those reassurances come with a kick in the pants to keep everyone squarely on the path of God's good graces.

There are two key points I want to convey. First, the themes I've just described are not confined to certain writings that scholars call "apocalypses," like Daniel 7–12, Revelation, and numerous other books that were widely read around the time of Jesus but mostly never made it into Jewish or Christian Bibles. Other ancient writings, including the great majority of the New Testament writings, also express those "apocalyptic" *themes*, even if they don't include, say, a tour of heaven or depictions of beasts with multiple heads. Second, the worldview on display in this literature is relatively consistent, suggesting that what I've described captures some of the ways that certain Jews in the first century were thinking about God, the world, the future, and what's possible.

Too many Christians get too excited about the Book of Revelation and read it in unhelpful ways, so I need to add: These apocalypses and their stock themes are not road maps or coded scripts meant to predict specific events or calamities to whoever figures out the "right" way to decipher them. They won't tell you when Jesus is coming back, what stocks to buy, when a new pandemic might arrive, or other similarly useful advice. These books tell us about the spiritual headwaters that fed streams in Judaism and the church. In those apocalyptic currents, we can detect at least two primary messages they were offering to ancient audiences living under the heel of foreign empires. First, don't expect an easy road. We live in a perilous world that suffers all kinds of distress. I mean the sorts of experiences that we today might chalk up to natural causes, political malfeasance, social hostility, or humanity's thirst for war. Second, God is faithful and will yet again prove faithful. Even when all the evidence around us might make us conclude that God is overwhelmed or too distracted to care about us, nevertheless, God is about to break in and set the world to rights. You just need to perceive what the revealer in the book has seen and respond accordingly.

Perhaps right now you are thinking one of the best questions anyone can ask when a conversation is about God and the Bible: *So what?*

I'm glad you asked.

The Gospels—especially Matthew, Mark, and Luke—suggest that these apocalyptic themes were woven through Jesus's teachings not because he was itching for widespread disaster but because he presented himself as a teacher (or a prophet) who had something to reveal about God's commitment to the world (all the world) and the world's future. Moreover, the Gospel authors, in the ways they present memories of Jesus, situate him among those apocalyptic ideas, because to the earliest believers he "fit" with those kinds of language, warnings, and hopes. To understand Jesus well, we need to know a bit about the waters from which he and his listeners drank. Finally, the Gospels frankly admit that God's work has not reached its end; life remains difficult. Even with all the joy and newness that comes with declaring, "Christ the Savior is born!" at Christmas, "Christ is risen!" at Easter, and nothing "will be able to separate us from the love of God in Christ Jesus our Lord" (Romans 8:39) all year round, still the Gospels admit that God has a job to finish. At least as long as our world and communities strain under all the hardships that make life dangerous, unjust, and grief-stricken, we should expect more from God, and we can.

Apocalyptic themes and longings provided a familiar way for Jesus and his followers to express all of that. Those ideas and hopes influence Jesus's perspectives on his work's urgency and the world's needs.

SETTING THE (BLEAK) SCENE FOR JESUS'S RETURN IN POWER AND GLORY

The Gospels of Matthew, Mark, and Luke all include a similar scene, although each book recounts it in a particular way. The scene consists of a speech Jesus gives to inform his followers about what they can expect in the future, and it culminates in him describing his eventual return to the earth in "power" and "glory." In all of these Gospels, the scene transpires in Jerusalem. Jesus is about to celebrate the first night of Passover with his people. His arrest occurs before the sun rises in the morning, just hours after the Passover dinner he shares with them. Prior to the speech in question, Jesus teaches in the Temple, as described by a series of episodes, placed one after the other, in which he either debates or criticizes different groups of Jewish religious leaders. We get indications of their frustrations and the delight of the crowd that witnesses Jesus holding forth (Matthew 21:23–23:39; Mark 11:27–12:44; Luke 19:47–21:4). Jesus's public display comes across as the last straw for the highest-ranking priests, who are the ones who will finally hand Jesus over to the Roman governor, Pontius Pilate, who has him crucified.

According to each of these three Gospels, the speech comes because people around Jesus point out the magnificence of the Temple complex in Jerusalem, which was an eye-popping architectural accomplishment adorned with precious metals and jewels. Jesus responds with an air of disdain, assuring everyone that the Temple will be cast down, leaving not one of its stones atop another one. Maybe that sounds preposterous to the people who hear him, maybe not. No one asks him how such comprehensive destruction could happen. Instead, they question him about when it will happen and what "sign" should they look for as a reliable indicator or warning (Matthew 24:1-3; Mark 13:1-4; Luke 21:5-7).

The topic of the Temple's demolition certainly interested the Gospels' original ancient audiences, for they lived between one and three decades after it actually happened in 70 CE (or, in the case of Mark, probably very soon after). Roman forces leveled the Temple complex as they put down a devastating revolt among Jews in Judea during the years 66–70, approximately forty years after Jesus's public ministry.

Jesus's speech offers his answer to the questions put to him about timing and "signs," although he does not exactly provide the specific information his questioners requested. In fact, he doesn't explicitly name the Temple at all but instead mostly talks about destruction and risk more generally.[3] The Gospels aren't implying that Jesus doesn't care about the Temple in particular. It's reasonable to assume that the original audiences of the Gospels would deduce that Jesus's words about widespread harm and ruin have a connection to the revolt of 66–70, which was effectively crushed on the day when the Romans looted, torched, and razed the Temple. Because Jesus remains relatively unspecific, however, we might experience his speech as also describing larger and recurring patterns of peril and conflict in the world.

Given where Jesus's speech fits in the narratives and the gravity of its subject matter, these Gospels are clearly accentuating the importance of what Jesus has to say. There is little narrative clutter after the speech. It is one of the last things Jesus shares with his admirers while he is still a free man. As we will see, he leaves them with reassurance that his imminent absence from them and the travails to come do not mean that he is abandoning them.

It sounds trite when someone asks you in a job interview, "Where do you see yourself in five years?" You're supposed to respond with something impressive and positive. Jesus's speech could be titled, "Here's where I see all of you in five years." And it's scary. The themes include many frightening apocalyptic elements, such as the reality of strife and the need for endurance in the face of opposition before God breaks in to make a change.

Jesus describes a future in which people have to guard against counterfeit Messiahs—religious charlatans (Matthew 24:4-28; Mark 13:5-23; Luke 21:8-24). Depending on which Gospel you're reading, Jesus says that there will be wars, famines, earthquakes, plagues, persecution, suffering, families violently turning on their own members, and additional deceptive religious prophets and leaders. As Matthew 24:12 poignantly puts it, "The love of many will grow cold." I already mentioned that those images describe bloodshed and panic during the revolt of 66–70. At the same time, on some days they sound eerily familiar. I wonder whether Jesus has been looking at the news feed on my phone.

Then again, all of it becomes familiar to Jesus too. Soon after this scene, especially in Mark's Gospel, the account of Jesus's crucifixion recalls some of the terms and images he uses here. The Gospel authors direct us to understand that Jesus himself participates in the agonies he describes as part of what it means to dwell in this world.

Through all of the adversities and distress, Jesus urges his hearers to endure, promising them that salvation awaits them when they do. He describes the turmoil as the time for his followers to take a stand. In a fraying world, they are to proclaim the good news about him (Matthew 24:14; Mark 13:10) and bear witness to what they know to be true (Luke 21:13). They will have work to do. It's as though the church rediscovers its true purpose when things are at their worst. That's a lesson for Christians in any era. Jesus warns about hardship to come because he wants his followers to be alert and ready for it, not so they will withdraw and focus on self-preservation, but so they will engage the world and take a stand for the love and kindness they have experienced in Jesus Christ.

Only after he describes all of that does he finally turn his attention to his return, which we will explore shortly.

Probably the song that's *least* likely to be playing in the back of your head right now is "It's Beginning to Look a Lot Like Christmas." We'll get to the Christmas stories before we reach the end of this book, fear not. Nevertheless, a valid question remains: What does this entire and severe apocalyptic speech from Jesus have to do with Advent and hope, anyway?

First, the scene makes a statement about a truth that we also rediscover and re-declare at Christmas every year: Our hope depends on God's commitment to the world. God expressed that commitment when God first "became flesh and lived among us" (John 1:14, part of a passage we will explore in chapter 3). We expect God to express it again, because injustice and suffering remain a part of our shared humanity. If God once bridged a distance that might have been said to keep heaven apart from earth, God will do it again. And again.

Second, as glorious as Christmas is, the arrival of Jesus in Bethlehem did not fix everything or remake the world into a safe, harmonious place. Our planet seems hardwired for disasters, and our poor stewardship of the environment makes everything worse. Humanity seems unable to tame its tendencies for violence and seeking dominance over others. Religion offers great comfort, but we still need to beware of manipulative wolves in sheep's clothing.

Read the news on any day: Love grows cold. As I'll explain further in chapter 2, Advent is, among other things, a season in which we can be honest about our discontent with the ongoing brokenness of our world and societies. Just like ancient apocalyptic ways of thinking were trying to buttress people's faith in God during times when they experienced acute oppression and disappointment, in Advent we remind ourselves that God has not and will not abandon us. Yet in Advent we also admit that we'd very much like to experience God keeping those promises about establishing a peaceable kingdom and a beloved community—hopefully soon.

Third, while we wait for the Messiah's arrival (or "advent"), our role is to bear witness to the good news of new life and divine mercy in Jesus Christ. Christians don't just *celebrate* Advent. In a way, our entire religion is an Advent religion. What I mean is we exist in a sort of perpetual state of waiting and hoping. God has done and shown us enough already in Jesus Christ, but we still await the finality and fullness of it all. We don't do that passively. Christian faith isn't like sitting in a waiting room. It's not so linear, like working our way through time. We're waiting for more to come from God, but we're also at the same time learning to recognize Christ already among us (or having already transformed us) because of his first advent at the first Christmas. Part of the "active hope" and "active waiting" I described in the introduction consists of Christians ourselves being a voice (and active agents) in the world for hope and compassion— not building anticipation for those things but expressing them now. Advent and Christmas are occasions to tell others about the power of the contagious hope within us. It's never too early in the season to start singing, "Go Tell It on the Mountain."

Finally, Jesus's speech, with all of its mention of hardship, never shows us the other side of the threshold. He does not motivate his hearers with descriptions of the justice, joy, reconciliation, and security that will come. There's no explicit promise of a new state of affairs, only the promise of a coming person: Jesus himself. We have to infer, from other parts of the Bible, the wonders of the salvation that Jesus will institute. For now, however, the person has to be enough. Before Advent is hope for any*thing*, it is hope for Jesus. Before hoping for some kind of *parousia*, or presentation of personal rewards, or culmination of God's intentions, we hope for Jesus. Advent hope is not hope in ideals, statistics, or policies; it's hope in a person, a relatable God, who is the embodiment of love, justice, mercy, and acceptance.

MARK 13:24-37

The evidence strongly suggest that Mark was written before the other Gospels, and that the authors of Matthew and Luke had access to it when they wrote, so let's begin with the details in its version of what Jesus says about his future return. We're about to explore complicated passages with many elements crying out for explanation, but for the specific focus of our investigation I will highlight only selected pieces of each one. Also, certain elements of what Jesus says appear in more than one Gospel. By the end, we will have a greater sense of how all three of them together can inform our outlook on Advent.

Jesus situates his return "after" the vast suffering he just described, which I've summarized. He's asked for a sign, and now at last he mentions a few of them that seem hard to miss. They aren't predictive signs. They serve as confirmations of Jesus's power and identity.

Alluding to a number of passages from the Old Testament describing cosmic upheaval, Jesus speaks of changes in the heavens. The reliability of sunlight, moonlight, and starlight will be altered.

These are not forecasts of specific eclipses (which scientists can now predict accurately) or meteor showers. Some in the ancient world viewed heavenly bodies as representatives of supernatural powers and reflections of armies. Jesus is speaking about the powers of the universe being realigned and the nations of this world becoming minimized in the face of a superior power becoming revealed. The Bible sees this kind of disruption as a signal of God's presence. We might celebrate the Messiah's humble birth at Christmas, but Jesus is painting a picture of a much more powerful, visible, and unmistakable arrival.

His reference to "the Son of Man coming in clouds" (a reference to Daniel 7:13) raises the stakes. Jesus speaks about himself with the expression *the Son of Man* (*the Human One* and *the Son of Humanity* are other good translations), and the mention of clouds also has a symbolic meaning. Clouds in the Bible (see, for example, Mark 9:7) and in other apocalyptic writings signify God's presence. Remember how the visit of a Roman dignitary might be considered a *parousia*? Jesus promises an event unlike any other in its grandeur—a divine manifestation or arrival. All the world, everyone from every corner of creation, will be gathered to encounter this.

Notice what is not here: no threats of punishment, no mention of people being taken away or booted out (only gathered), and no sense of wrath. Given the wider context of Jesus's speech, this scene appears to bring about the end of the strife and terror that he has already discussed. God's power will one day put an end to all of that, quashing whatever creates misery and hinders the world's flourishing. Hoping for such a time is also part of Advent.

I mentioned earlier that different Christians expect different things in response to Jesus's promises of his future return. That is due partially to the symbolic character of what he says. He doesn't offer a clear script. Some of the differing opinions come from the passage of time, especially since Jesus also says that all these developments will occur before "this generation" passes away. Statements like that appear differently in the rearview mirror of history, especially as they fade farther into the past. Taking the passage excessively literally ties us in knots. This is not just a modern observation, for we see even in the New Testament itself different opinions about how to live in light of our hope in the future that Jesus has in mind. Advent themes usually accent the promise of Jesus's return and the arrival of a time of reckoning. Some biblical voices emphasize instead the value of living now with an awareness that we've already been raised up with Christ (see, for example, Colossians 3:1-3).

It's worth pausing to note the effects of teachers and preachers who weaponize passages like this one. I regularly encounter seminary students and folks in congregations with awful stories to tell about being terrorized by passages about Jesus's return, as if those parts of the Bible are meant to be threats more than reassurances. Some of this has to do with misunderstandings about where the New Testament's apocalyptic motifs came from. Some of it has to do with just mean ways of using the Bible to control people and stoke fear.

However you respond to this passage, or whatever memories it might unearth within you, I hope you can sense in it a promise of a better future and a remade world. Jesus doesn't talk about specifics on the other side, like streets of gold, scallops for dinner every night, or the end of Parkinson's disease. But he does intimate that the powers of this world that wreck lives and the creation (that is, the world's systems, hatreds, fears, oppressors, and more) are not absolute. They will not last forever.

Part of Advent involves reflecting on what you're hoping for. What do you expect God to do? What kind of future do you hope to live in? What's your role in bearing witness about it, in words and deeds?

In Mark, Jesus ends his speech with a call to "keep awake" (*Wachet auf!*). He's not saying that people are going to be in big trouble if they aren't paying attention when God does something big. Instead, he doesn't want anyone to opt out of eagerly watching, longing, and preparing for it. Even while waiting and persevering, his followers have something to say in a weary world.

MATTHEW 24:29-44

Matthew's account of Jesus's speech is longer than Mark's, although it incorporates much of what Mark says, particularly in Matthew 24:29-35. Most notable among the differences is Jesus's extended reflection on the fact that no one knows the timing of his future return, including "the angels of heaven" and himself. Only God (the one Jesus calls "Father") knows. Jesus cannot and so will not answer the question his disciples put to him in the first place, prompting this speech: "When will this be?" (Matthew 24:3). He would rather impress upon them the unpredictability of it all.

Just as life continued as it always had prior to the great Flood that destroyed life on the earth (according to the tale told in Genesis 6:11–7:24), so too Jesus's return will come and take many by surprise. Part of the rhetoric here is motivational; Jesus implicitly commends Noah for being prepared for the rain because he was responsive to God's instructions. Jesus's followers should likewise be prepared and "keep awake" and alert.

Jesus highlights activities from humanity's normal affairs: people working in a field or grinding grain with no special insight that they stand on the verge of a new future. Only God knows what will happen, and apparently there is no clear sign that a given day is nearer to or further from the fulfillment of God's promises than any other day. It's unpredictable.

We aren't told what it means that some are "taken" and others are "left." A sorting is taking place, which is consistent with other things Jesus says in this part of Matthew (for example, Matthew 25:1-13, 31-46). Jesus doesn't specify whether it's better to be left or taken. That isn't the purpose of this passage. It's not a diagram of the afterlife. Instead, Jesus appears more interested in instilling a sense of urgent watchfulness in his followers.

Still, that has not prevented some Christians from stretching this passage to mean more than it says. More than a few preachers and teachers use it to support an understanding that Jesus will someday whisk away all the true believers from the face of the earth, so everyone else will be left behind to fend for themselves in a dangerous social and political landscape. It would require a separate book for me to explain everything that is problematic and deceptive about the idea that there will be a "rapture" in which Jesus snatches folks away without warning, launching an era of chaos and fear. Let me only say plainly that those ideas stem from an outlook on the Bible that has to twist Scripture into flimsy distortions and supply connections among a range of verses that otherwise appear unconnected. It's an outlook full of presumptions that one particular slice of the Christian church has everything right about God and everyone else in the world deserves to be punished. Maybe most concerning, it's a view that seems eager to ascribe unusual cruelty to God. It certainly imports all kinds of assumptions into this passage, turning it into a prediction of divine terror instead of a reassurance of God's intention to redeem and heal the world. It's a perspective that distorts the Bible. Worse, it distorts the love of God.

The divisions drawn in this passage remain concerning, nevertheless. The passage operates according to a dualism, meaning it splits people into two and only two exclusive categories, the taken and the undisturbed. That dualistic way of thinking is common in the apocalyptic writings I explained earlier. It can be a useful way to get people's attention and to encourage good behavior, just like the old cartoons when someone facing a decision has an angel on one shoulder and a demon on the other, both whispering into an ear. Yet real life is more complicated than that, and plenty of other biblical passages point out the destruction caused when human beings think that they can divide the world into the saints and the sinners or the insiders and the outsiders. Apocalyptic ways of describing the world and the work of God have their limits. Their intensity allows them to arrest people's attention, but we also need other ways of speaking about God and God's ways of interacting with humanity.

In chapter 2 we will take a deeper look at the topic of judgment and how some voices from the Bible suggest that the arrival of the Messiah means a reckoning will occur. For now, however, we should note that this passage from Matthew counsels readers *not* to presume that they can or should make judgments among humanity. After all, the passage suggests that there's nothing apparently different about the two people in the field or the two grinding grain. The distinctions that this passage talks about are only God's to make.

Despite the disturbing elements of this passage, I appreciate the ways it commends attentiveness and vigilance—good Advent themes. Part of Christian faith involves cultivating a keen sense of our dependence on God, whether life is going smoothly or not. Faith is not a promise of power we receive that lets us lord ourselves over others or retreat from the world and its needs. Attentiveness to God will produce attentiveness to our neighbors. Attentiveness to our neighbors will produce attentiveness to their needs and struggles, even as it produces appreciation for who they are as people made in God's image. Christian faith is about more than believing and knowing.

It's about opening ourselves up to God and others, responding to our neighbors with compassion, and finding hope from internalizing the loving-kindness that God shows to everyone, without exceptions.

LUKE 21:25-36

The Gospels don't pretend to offer precise transcripts of Jesus's speeches and sayings. They are trying to convey Jesus's general character and the essence of his teachings. We shouldn't be surprised, then, that Luke's version of this episode has some notable differences from the others.

Jesus refers to his future return "with power and great glory" by likewise citing Daniel 7:13 and its imagery of a divinely authorized and divinely accompanied "Son of Man," whom the Gospels identify as Jesus. Differences in Luke's version emerge when Jesus has more to say here about cosmic "signs" or indicators, as well as the sense of danger people feel in response to them and other instances of upheaval in the natural world. It's a scary scene, in its own way.

Jesus nevertheless instructs his hearers to respond positively, because it all means that "your redemption is drawing near." In other words, this is an ultimate act—not necessarily "ultimate" in the sense of "final" or "concluding" but in the sense of "culminating" or "perfecting." The Messiah comes to complete a task: salvation. As we will see in chapters 3 and 4, people in Luke have been awaiting that completion ever since the opening chapters of his Gospel. Advent expectation begins in Luke when Elizabeth and Mary become pregnant. It will conclude when the world's ultimate redemption finally arrives.

Jesus also tells a parable that recalls one in Mark 13:28-31 and Matthew 24:32-35. He concludes by encouraging everyone to remain "on guard" and "alert." To keep us on track in our study of Advent hope, I'll devote extended time to reflecting on the first paragraph in this passage, verses 25-28.

Reading the Bible is always a cross-cultural exercise, for we encounter in its pages different moral norms, cultural practices, and ways of understanding the universe. We can learn a lot about the assumptions that ancient readers and hearers carried with them when they encountered the writings of the Bible. It takes some imagination, however, to find ways for the Bible's symbols and hopes to address us, given our modern understandings. This paragraph from Luke offers a good place to practice that.

Today we have explanations for phenomena such as changes in the heavens, earthquakes, and violent weather. Stars explode and new ones are born, and tools like the James Webb Space Telescope give us clearer insight into those stunning processes than anyone before us had. Earthquakes are not expressions of divine anger; tectonic plates move and slip, releasing pressure that sends enormous amounts of energy across the surface of the earth where we reside. We are learning—hopefully not too late—humanity's own contributions to intense storms and rising seas. We have ways of understanding what makes our lives vulnerable and fleeting in the grand scheme of the universe, even if we can't stop it.

Moreover, we know that the world experiences change and distress because of dynamics that are built into existence itself. Species evolve. Continents drift. And, of course, some of those changes can have wide-ranging consequences for human well-being. Volcanoes erupt. Hurricanes form. The dinosaurs would like to have a word about the problem with asteroids.

I'm not celebrating or minimizing the harmful dimensions of this world that we cannot control. I'm saying that they remain part of our lives, yet they are not a part of life that invalidates God's promises or God's reliability. I understand the reasons why people ask, "If God exists, and if God is loving, why are there tsunamis?" Or, less newsworthy but often more devastating, "Doesn't God want to heal my child's leukemia?" No one can give satisfactory answers to those questions. I know that suffering can make it difficult or impossible for people to have any faith at all. I merely want to acknowledge that life is unfair and suffering is rampant. As a result, a question like this becomes all the more urgent and potentially transformative: What difference could it make for a world like ours if we nevertheless believe that God is committed to human flourishing and wholeness? And: If I indeed believe that to be true about God, how am I compelled to hope and to offer help to others?

What Jesus describes in this passage is not God's desire to damage the planet or to hurt anyone. We hear Jesus's voice describing the way things just are, both for his ancient audiences and for us. The world exists in a state of flux, as do our lives. The natural world is simultaneously beautiful and dangerous. I grew up a short drive from Half Moon Bay, California, which sits on the Pacific Ocean. I've seen amazing sunsets. I also know what can happen if you turn your back on the surf. Jesus declares that all of the instability and peril around us are not signs of God's indifference. It's where we live, and God can be found here even now, among us in the throes, as we live in light of God's ultimate redemption.

The good news residing at the heart of Christian faith does not promise to scoop us up out of a precarious existence or to makes us immune from every threat, at least not yet. But it does promise that God is reliable, even in the midst of so much uncertainty. God will never forget about us. The Bible doesn't tell us why the world is as it is, at least not with the amount of detail I'd like, but it does tell us that God will meet us here.

That's a voice I hear in the traditions, texts, and music of Advent, a declaration that redemption is coming. It's on its way. It seems to be in process already. Making predictions or assuming everything will naturally get better over time, or worse over time—all those approaches are misguided. Right now, we live in the fray, not above it. And the faithfulness of God toward us, toward our neighbors, and toward all creation is our North Star, a light that stays lit even when it can be difficult for us to see.

In Conclusion

Jesus's dramatic and foreboding descriptions about a future and culminating (re)arrival are not a script leaked to the public ahead of time nor itemized predictions from someone who knows every detail of a secret plan. He sketches faint images and evokes emotions to kick start our anticipation for a refashioned world.

Remember that this speech begins because people ask Jesus to supply them with knowledge and privileged insight about the future. He gives them something else instead. He provides reassurance of God's faithfulness. It's a faithfulness to be demonstrated yet again in Jesus's future coming, his promise of a powerful transformation of our reality. He also imparts instructions about how his followers should conduct themselves courageously and faithfully in an unraveling world. Those instructions are the part that resides within our grasp and within the bounds of what we can envision.

If we transport what Jesus says in this speech to our reflections during Advent, we might say that the arrivals of Jesus that we celebrate and expect are not opportunities for us to receive and wield special wisdom. Rather, in encountering Jesus we discover opportunities to live in freedom and generosity, which grow out of our confidence

23

in God's reliability and love. Faith finds ways to speak hope into difficulties and does not shrink from challenges.

Fortunately, this faith we're talking about is more than a virtue inside of me or you. It's something shared by the whole church and, locally, a specific community of believers. We navigate the world Jesus describes together. We don't have to do it alone. Advent hope, like faith itself, is a team effort.

In Advent we remember promises God has made, and we look forward to seeing God make good on them and fulfill them. Some of those promises are grand. We're talking about much more than God's sunny companionship throughout our lives. When Jesus chooses apocalyptic language and symbols to voice his outlook on the world and its eventual redemption, he announces that there's something a little subversive, too, about the promise of his *parousia*. That means there's something similarly subversive about his nativity at Christmas. (In chapter 3 we will explore how his mother expresses her own awareness of this.) The subversive element is that God loves the world too much to let it go its own way. How exactly the future will play out remains unknown. This, however, is certain: Love won't stay cold forever.

We can observe Advent in a binocular way, training one eye on the fragility and wonder of childbirth (Christmas) and one on the expectation that Jesus will somehow complete the healing of the world in a display of power and glory (his future re-arrival). When we do so we discover that we aren't talking about two disconnected, self-contained events with a very long and lengthening pause between them. Rather, Christmas sets redemption in motion, establishing it, then planting it like a seed, until it comes full flower. The work is already done; it happens at Christmas. But it's also not yet done. It's underway but we expect more, and we need more. *Already* and *not yet*—both can be true at once.

Advent gives us an opportunity to know that our redemption is both already underway and not yet complete—not because we're tasked to solve the mysteries of the universe first, but because we're told to pay attention to God's commitment to accompany us. We stay alert to who God has called us to be and what God has called us to do. We are agents of God's subversive intentions.

And so we begin Advent by clearing the sleep from our eyes and recognizing a voice that might sound familiar. "Wake up, the voice calls to us," as Bach reminds us. The voice belongs to Jesus Christ, who does more than call to us. The Messiah also calls us—to endure and to join in his efforts.

CHAPTER 2

THE VOICE OF JOHN THE BAPTIST

Preparing the Way of the Lord

Passages We Will Explore:

- Mark 1:1-8
- Matthew 3:1-12
- Luke 3:1-18
- John 1:6-8, 19-34
- Matthew 11:2-11

If you don't know what the Isenheim Altarpiece is (and most people don't, so don't worry), search for it online and take a look. In the center of this large work is a grim depiction of Jesus's crucifixion, painted in the early sixteenth century by Matthias Grünewald. It offers a rather accurate visual summary of the main thing that the New Testament writers want you to know about John the Baptist.

On the Altarpiece, John is the one on the right side of the cross, from our perspective. He's wearing little more than a red tunic lined with fur, holding a book, and pointing a rather long index finger straight at Jesus's corpse. Next to John, Grünewald painted the words

27

of John 3:30 (in Latin), in which John declares, "He must increase, but I must decrease." The painting involves a lot of imagination, mostly because John himself had been executed before Jesus was. It nevertheless captures the Gospels' main point about John the Baptist: He is the one designated to bear witness to the emergence of God's Messiah.

The Altarpiece's depiction of John identifying a crucified man and not a charismatic teacher or healer as God's deliverer is purposely shocking. At the beginning of multiple Gospels, before Jesus begins his public ministry, John tells his listeners that they should expect someone "more powerful" than he (Matthew 3:11; Mark 1:7; Luke 3:16). Yet that man ends up killed in a horrific manner on Good Friday. Hanging on a cross is about the most powerless posture one can imagine. According to Grünewald's outlook, that's part of the point, yet John's testimony remains true through time, whether Jesus is preaching, dying, or manifesting a resurrected body. Sometimes God's arrival and God's power don't match what we might expect. People like John urge us to examine everything more closely.

In this chapter we will explore what John the Baptist has to say about the Christ and how we should prepare for his coming. The Gospels present John's testimony about Jesus as significant. John's voice extends beyond telling people gathered at the Jordan River in the first century CE *that* the Christ will soon appear. John also announces what everyone should expect from that arrival. John helps us know more about what kind of Christ to expect as we continue reading the Gospels.

WHO IS THIS GUY?

John the Baptist is one of the most peculiar figures in the Bible, and that's saying something. (You are welcome to call him John the

Baptizer if you prefer. He lived far before there were such things as Baptists and other Christian denominations.) John remains a bit of a mystery. In the Bible, only Luke 1:5-25 tells about his extraordinary origins, saying he was born to a childless couple who had been unable to conceive children and were "both were getting on in years," to put it diplomatically (Luke 1:7). After John's birth, his father speaks a prophecy about him, which we will explore in chapter 3. We learn nothing else about John until we meet him as an adult, in all four Gospels, teaching and baptizing people in a wilderness region. He attracts crowds. He ends up executed. His followers outlive him (according to Acts 19:1-7).

Learning more about John and the significance of what he was doing in the wilderness allows us to enter John's time and place. Doing so provides clearer insight into what he says. We will also discover that there were ways in which John might have done even more than what the Gospels focus on—that is, identifying Jesus. He probably influenced Jesus and his message as well, as the Gospels suggest. For example, Matthew puts both John's preaching and Jesus's in parallel, saying that each of them announces the nearness of God's "kingdom" (Matthew 3:2; 4:17). In John's Gospel, Jesus's disciples (evidently under Jesus's direction) also baptize people (John 3:22-28; 4:1-2). Jesus therefore endorses what John did and taught; maybe Jesus even models his own message after John's.

In addition to the Gospels, there are Christian writings from several decades later that talk about John's deeds and influence, but the stories they tell have a rather legendary air about them. At the very least, their sheer existence establishes that people have always been interested in John and his religious imagination. Perhaps curiosity about John is more intense because so little information about him has survived, leading us to conclude that there's a larger story to tell about someone who was clearly a renowned, influential, and controversial public figure. Even the Qur'an (seventh century CE) refers to John a few times, with the Arabic name Yahya, and considers him a prophet. So, who was he?

An ancient Jewish historian named Josephus offers a few sentences about John in his work *Antiquities of the Jews*, written in the mid- 90s CE, around the same time as the Gospels.[1] Josephus confirms some basic aspects of John's life that the Gospels also note, saying that John was popular, led people to participate in a baptismal ritual, and was executed by Herod Antipas. Josephus claims that Herod Antipas feared that John's popularity and the zeal of his followers were too combustible and could end up triggering an insurrection. There's no reason, then, to doubt that John existed and was a religious reformer. All in all, we know John's out there, in history. At the same time, he—or, at least key details about his life—remains fairly opaque to us.

Scholars debate how much we can actually know about John. We have only limited evidence about him. It's also apparent that the New Testament creates distorted perspectives about John because it devotes so much effort (as we will see shortly) toward integrating him with Jesus. We can suspect that John did more with his days than just wait around for Jesus to show up so he could point that long metaphorical finger at him. What was John preparing for, and why would anyone listen to his voice? We can answer those questions when we dig into what we know about John's world.

Most likely John began preaching to others around 27–29 CE, which would align with what we read in Luke 3:1-2, that "the word of God came to" him during "the fifteenth year of the reign of Tiberius Caesar." (The range of possible years reflects disagreement about what specific event was considered the starting point of Tiberius's ascension to emperor. There are always uncertainties that lead historians to quibble.) John's execution occurred probably in 29 or 30 CE. Like the Messiah who followed him, he could not elude for long the powerful people who considered him and his teachings dangerous to the social stability that Rome demanded.

A water ritual was the hallmark of John's religious message. The Greek word from which we get the English *baptism* and *baptize* means "dipping." John was not unique, however, for there were plenty of water-based purification rites (the fancy name is *lustrations*) in Judaism and other religions during his time. In other words, dunking people in a river does not mean anything on its own; the question is why to do it and what it symbolizes. Josephus says John employed a baptism for the purification of one's body, while the Gospels tend to describe it as "a baptism of repentance for the forgiveness of sins" (Mark 1:4; Luke 3:3; note that Matthew 3:11 says the baptism is just "for repentance").

Maybe the most interesting thing about this baptism is that the descriptions of it incorporate religious dynamics and language that many of John's Jewish contemporaries would have associated with the Temple in Jerusalem and the rituals that priests conducted there. John does not appear to be using baptism as a way of urging people to spend time at the Temple but instead as a kind of alternative ritual in an alternative location. We have reason to suppose, then, that John might have seen his own wilderness ministry as a substitute for—if not a replacement of—the Jerusalem temple and its priesthood. When Sadducees, a group that includes the elite chief priests in Jerusalem, come to John for baptism in Matthew 3:7, the event could cast doubt on whether we should see John's ministry as a rival to the Temple operations, but at the same time, John hardly welcomes those prominent leaders with open arms. Perhaps Jesus learned some of his own criticisms of the Temple's leadership from John (see, for example, Mark 11:15-17; John 2:13-22).

Ironically enough, John's father, Zechariah, was a priest (according to Luke 1:5). Not only does John appear uninterested in entering the family business, so to speak, he possibly was setting up his own alternative! None of this indicates, however, that John was abandoning Judaism or yearning for a Messiah who would do so. We can fairly surmise that John saw himself as repairing Judaism or at least some aspects of it, probably by criticizing the current priesthood more than he was repudiating the notion of a physical temple and its rituals.

The information we have about John also confirms that he was sympathetic to, if not closely aligned with, a community of people called Essenes. The label *Essenes* encompasses a wide range of Jewish groups from the period. We know about them through archaeology, Josephus, and the writings that some of them composed. It is unwise to get too specific about which Essene group(s) John might have participated in or learned from, but nevertheless Josephus's description of him has some connections with what the historian says elsewhere about Essenes. Many Essenes lived in communities away from population centers, which tracks with what the Gospels say about John residing in "the wilderness" and near the Jordan River. Some of those Essene groups—most famously the one situated at Qumran, which left behind the Dead Sea Scrolls—were outright hostile toward the leadership of the Jerusalem temple and believed that their own isolated Essene communities and rituals constituted a new, embodied, and spiritualized temple. A number of their writings anticipate that God would soon purge the world of wickedness and usher in a new era of righteousness. John, then, was probably influenced by those beliefs. Accordingly, he could have been both out of patience with the priestly elite in Jerusalem and very passionate in his expectation that God's ways would come to fruition in a dramatic, God-initiated fashion.

Finally, if you haven't already made the connection in your own mind, notice that there are similarities between what I've just described about Essenes and the apocalyptic perspectives we encountered in chapter 1. From the basic contours I've sketched so far, John appears right at home in that environment of charged expectations. When the Gospels depict him proclaiming that God is about to bring judgment to the world, think of that judgment as accomplishing *change* more than *destruction*. John expects transformation through a show of strength on God's part. His voice sounds fed up with the way things are, and he is eager to help people be ready for the newness he expects God will soon unleash.

MARK 1:1-8

Remember that Mark was the first of the Bible's Gospels to be written. That doesn't make it better or worse than the other three, but sometimes it means Mark is briefer when it comes to describing a person or a scene. Matthew and Luke often take what Mark says in a given place and add to it. Mark is also in general more abrupt and unwilling to give much detail or explanation.

This Gospel gets right to the point, beginning the whole story of Jesus with a short description of John. Mark's opening words draw from the Old Testament to give us a sense of John's significance. A combination of passages—blending Isaiah 40:3; Exodus 23:20; and Malachi 3:1—associates John with old promises about God making a way for a return. The imagery conjures the idea of a road (a "way") that has been made clearer to follow or safer to travel. The road symbolizes restoration and the accomplishment of God's purposes. Later Mark will indicate Jesus and his followers travel on a "way" leading to Jerusalem and his execution (Mark 9:33; 10:32, 52).

Mark situates John "in the wilderness," out in the desert where food and water can be scarce. When resources are limited, we might feel our dependence on God in acute ways. Accordingly, John lives off the land, opting for a diet of bugs and honey. Around John's time, some of the Jewish Essenes at Qumran and perhaps elsewhere viewed the wilderness as the place where God had directed them to prepare themselves for God to turn the page to a new era in history.

The demanding conditions of the desert also recall memories of other wilderness experiences in the Bible, such as Moses's initial encounter with God at the burning bush (Exodus 3:1-6), the Hebrews' ongoing struggles and formation before they entered the land to which God directed them, and Isaiah's promises of the desert one day blossoming like a flower when God leads people home from their exile (Isaiah 35:1). The desert is a desolate yet living reminder that God tends to show up in out-of-the-way places and out-of-the-way processes. The wilderness holds surprises. That seems fitting for Advent, because Jesus's arrival will not look like the birth of a conventional king or hero. He'll be born on the edges—laid to rest in a manger, then taken by his parents to Egypt as political refugees.

When we read about John's clothing we should pause. Sometimes every detail of the narrative matters, and rarely does the Bible comment on people's outfits. The fur John wears in Grünewald's painting suggests that the artist had read Mark, for John wears camel's hair and a leather belt. This sounds like the prestigious prophet Elijah, who according to 2 Kings 1:8 was "a hairy man with a leather belt around his waist." Why would John style himself in a way to recall Elijah?

One possible answer to that question takes us back to the Old Testament Book of Malachi, which ends with a declaration that God will send Elijah back to earth "before the great and terrible day of the Lord comes" (Malachi 4:5-6). Elijah never dies in Scripture; God takes him directly into heaven in 2 Kings 2:11. Malachi proclaims that Elijah will be a forerunner of a time of divine judgment and restoration. I'm not suggesting that John thought he was Elijah reborn. He might, however, have been trying to prompt people to take him seriously and to recall memories about Elijah to express his own deep conviction that a time of God's reckoning was very near.[2]

Finally, John announces that someone "more powerful" is on the way and will offer a different sort of baptism, one that purifies or transforms through the power of the Holy Spirit. John does not explain what that means, but it implies an act of God—obviously something much more dramatic and life-changing than his ritual in the Jordan River.

John's voice in Mark, along with John's wardrobe and location, declares that a time of disruption is coming. John characterizes the public arrival of Jesus as an occasion marked by a divine intrusion and expressions of God's power. Something new and unmistakable is about to dawn, both in John's time and again for us every Advent, for in this season we anticipate Jesus among us once again, not just in past history but also in ongoing mystery. We can detect both warnings and reassurances in Mark's presentation of John. The disruption to come appears to be beyond humanity's control, yet it's good news. It creates a need for repentance, yet forgiveness is readily available. John's warnings and reassurances grow louder in what the other Gospels say about him.

MATTHEW 3:1-12

Matthew's introduction to John the Baptist looks familiar to us, now that we've explored Mark's. But, of course, we learn more when Matthew provides additional reports of the kinds of things John says.

If John has a soft side, Matthew seems uninterested in revealing it. Intense language appears throughout: There's a "coming wrath," an "ax" is ready to level fruitless trees so they can be burned, and the person coming after John will separate wheat from chaff. All of this speaks about a coming reckoning or judgment.

Maybe you've seen people who remind you of John and his rantings as they stand on busy streets and holler at passers-by to announce that God's judgment is imminent. We keep our heads down and repeat a mantra as we shuffle past: "Don't make eye contact. Don't make eye contact." I'm saying that John is easy to ignore as long as we convince ourselves that he's either unhinged or a proponent of "fire and brimstone" religion that we recognize as too mean, hypocritical, or abusive. But that would be to misunderstand John. (Plus, Jesus says similarly harsh things in the Gospels from time to time, so we still have to look up and deal with *those* at some point.)

When I teach I often encounter students who bristle when they hear the word *repentance*, which shows up occasionally in the New Testament and in this passage. The word has been used to scold and shame them, because it's been dropped on them as a kind of morality gauge, meant to convince them that they'll never measure up, never be pure enough, and never be worthy enough. For some of those students, constant calls for repentance have participated in wrecking their self-image. We need to take a closer look at what it means to "repent."

Many parts of the Bible teach us that we are all sinful, more so than we realize. We regularly turn from God's goodness as individuals and communities, and we benefit from God's forgiveness, which empowers us to go forward. Sometimes sin entails harming others, sometimes it's harming ourselves, and sometimes it looks more like apathy or not believing that we are worthy of the dignity we inherently possess. But all of that can be understood quite differently from the exclusively moralistic (or sanctimonious) way that some people issue demands for repentance. Those demands too often make it sound as if human beings are thoroughly rotten and have no capacity to do good.

The Greek word behind our English vocabulary about *repentance* does not refer to contrition or feeling self-blaming regret about one's behavior. It is not primarily about immorality, impurity, or a defective will. It's not a call to "Shape up!" Instead, its main meaning is about taking on a new perspective or a changed mind. It is a call to notice something you previously didn't or to adopt an altogether different point of view. It doesn't mean, "Come to your senses!" as much as it means, "See what's happening here, see what this really is. View it a new way and let that change things for you!" Granted, a changed point of view may lead to a sense of remorse and a desire to change one's behavior. I mean, there may be moral implications, and contrition might be appropriate after we contemplate the world or who we are in new light. First and foremost, however, "Repent!" is an invitation to open one's mind. That makes it a very appropriate word and activity for Advent. What changes in your mind when you consider that the Messiah is born among us—a long time ago, yes, but also again in our own ongoing spiritual journey? What difference can that make for us and for the world?

In his teachings, John urges the crowds to see what he sees and to understand what he understands. He begs them to perceive the great discrepancy between how things are and how things ought to be, in God's merciful assessment of our reality. John's message leads those who are convinced to respond by confessing their sins and undergoing baptism. They join John in the water because they join him in expecting what he expects. They prepare themselves to meet this "more powerful" person, this Messiah who will sort things out. Part of their activity involves *confessing*: They are telling the truth about themselves and the world. (Confession refers to admitting something and bringing it into the open, as if to say, "We all agree that this is how it is." The prefix *con-* indicates that this is an admission that happens together or with others. Collectively, and before God, we "*fess* up" about the world and our place in it.)

Bryan Stevenson, the founder and executive director of the Equal Justice Initiative and the author of the excellent book *Just Mercy*, is fond of insisting that truth always has to precede reconciliation.[3] We cannot repair the injustices in our world unless we first admit the truth about them and engage in some kind of communal confession. I think John the Baptist is up to something similar in his calls for repentance. He's not aiming to make everyone feel like worthless worms; he's aware that the world needs to be repaired, he believes that God is committed to the task, and he's inviting everyone to get ready.

John's not the most normal person you'll meet in the Bible, but don't dismiss him as a fanatical, feral, bug-eating oddball. His urgency and warnings reveal his exasperation about a society that isn't living up to what it can be or is being held back from being what it can be. Maybe this sounds familiar to you.

The imagery of a coming judgment in John's teachings makes many of us uncomfortable. One thing is clear, however: Any judgment that's going to happen is Jesus's responsibility and not John's or anyone else's. At the same time, I'm willing to chalk up some of John's fervor here as evidence of his growing discontentment, coming from his weariness with a world that doesn't match what he believes it could be, if only God would show up. John refuses to hold back.

I find John's voice strangely comforting during Advent because his anticipation of Jesus's arrival gives me permission to be a little dissatisfied with the world too. I don't know exactly what might have caused John to be dismayed or if he even was. But, like him, I long for God to fix the things in the world that I suspect bring sadness to God. There are so many ways we turn from what's good for us and deprive our neighbors of what they need to thrive. That doesn't lead me to talk about divine judgment like John, but it does make me impatient for lasting change to materialize. Then I have to acknowledge that I have other choices available to me besides sitting on my hands or fantasizing about an instantaneous divine act of cosmic housecleaning.

I sometimes wonder in Advent: "Are we still here? Are we still gathering around tiny flames on Advent wreaths as if they are beacons that can illuminate a new way forward?" We still live as though gun violence in schools is a cost we're willing to absorb. We still react to poverty and massive wealth inequality with indifference.

Hope is a mistake, if all our hope leads us to do today is stay huddled together or run away into the desert. Advent instead involves a different type of hope, one that has an active, restless character. Those candles on the wreaths do more than provide stubborn resistance against encroaching shadows. Flames in the Bible symbolize purification and wholeness. Moreover, they symbolize God's presence. The tiny fires contain more power than they appear to, for they become to me a lighthouse of that active hope, vaguely illuminating in my mind a future that I'm still trying to see. I'm repenting my way toward that future, so to speak. I'm trying to stay on the road toward it. It's a future in which God will keep promises, and I'm called to do what I can to be ready, because that future is already beginning.

You might find it helpful in Advent to reflect on where your hopes point. If you want, you can ponder what frustrates or angers you or what breaks your heart. Where do you want to see God's healing take place? Big issues are fine, such as alleviating world hunger, but let me encourage you also to identify something more local and something easier to wrap your head around. Maybe children in your city or town show up for school hungry, and there are programs that need funding or staffing to provide solutions. John the Baptist might say, "Well done, you've just confessed something. Now let's see if you can join in reconciling that problem, trusting God to help. That would be 'fruit worthy of repentance.'"

LUKE 3:1-18

Before we dig into Luke, I have a story. Several years ago, I had the opportunity to learn from a Jewish rabbinic scholar over a few days. On one occasion he offered a short reflection on part of the Torah, describing a few specific teachings as insightful for understanding what the whole Torah is about. He chose two verses that I admit I had never previously given much attention:

> *You shall have a designated area outside the camp to which you shall go. With your tools you shall have a trowel; when you relieve yourself outside, you shall dig a hole with it and then cover up your excrement.*
>
> *Deuteronomy 23:12-13*

You read that right. The passage describes a law for those dwelling in a military encampment, and its reference to a "trowel" might mean simply a tent peg or some other simple digging tool. I'm not sure you need a Bible scholar for more than that. The rest of the passage speaks for itself.

The rabbi said it is typical instruction for the Torah: Leave the world a better place than you found it (or, at least, don't leave it in worse condition). He extolled the simplicity of it all. As you go about your life, think of who is going to come (or "go"!) after you. In other words, righteous living is not necessarily about heroic action. It consists of the conscientious things we do daily. Be faithful. Be caring. Be merciful. Clean up your mess.

I often forget the simplicity, partly because Jesus's act of self-giving in his crucifixion occupies so much space in the New Testament, and the exploits of Peter and Paul get so much attention. Depending on your own denominational background, you might have been taught about martyrs and saints, or maybe someone told you that Mary the mother of Jesus should be your model for faithful living. So many biblical heroes set a high bar! It's true, however, that faithfulness is made up of daily actions and regular choices. Change and compassion begin there.

Now we come to Luke and its description of John the Baptist's public ministry and teaching in the Jordan River Valley. Luke repeats much of what Mark and Matthew say about John but with its own flourishes. I want to dwell in the part that is unique to this Gospel: Luke 3:10-14. Luke describes John interacting with a crowd, and they want specifics: "OK, fine, call us a 'brood of vipers' who need to change our outlook and get our act together. We believe you. But 'what, then, should we do?'"

John does not command them to live like him. He doesn't say, "Make yourself an itchy sweater out of fur, find your own beehive, and try these locusts—they're good if you dip them in oregano and olive oil." He doesn't require people to abandon the cities, their jobs, and their families. They aren't asked to preach or take any religious vows.

John teaches them to share their surplus clothing and food with people who lack those basic needs. It's the kind of stuff we all should be doing. (Easy to say, harder to do, I realize.) It's as obvious—and as understated—as the virtue of walking outside of camp to poop and using a shovel to cover it when you do.

Then tax collectors and soldiers arrive. Likely they are Jews, just like the rest of John's audience. Although Jewish, they make their living serving the occupying Roman Empire, squeezing as many coins as they can out of the colonizing enterprise and providing the muscle and blood that maintains business as usual by controlling the Judean locals. Some considered them traitors against their own people. Surely John, that outspoken voice against unrighteousness, is going to rail against them and the injustice that's built into the imperial system they support. Maybe he'll make them quit their jobs and perform some kind of penance. No. None of that happens. In contrast, John replies to them with words I find surprising, telling them simply to perform their work in a fair way. Tax collectors and soldiers in the Roman provinces enjoyed great latitude in being able to exploit their positions for personal gain. They could fleece their neighbors, often with no repercussions. John says, "Just do your job. Refuse the corruption and callousness that you can easily get away with. Act justly."

We've already noted that John's voice issues both warnings and reassurances as he anticipates the arrival of the Messiah. Luke includes warnings that we've seen in other Gospels too. The reassurance here is that you don't need to be a hero to be a part of God's efforts to restore the world.

Apparently, John knows that neither he nor any movement he might lead can create heaven on earth. John's not paralyzed by the magnitude of what we call structural or systemic injustice. He calls for resisting it through basic decency and faithfulness. We might extend this, then, and say that Advent isn't about perfecting yourself so you can be blameless before God and only then be prepared for God to work through you. Advent isn't about our attempts to purge all that corrupts the world. Advent and the promise of Christ's coming involve an invitation to enlist ourselves in his cause not by completing a long moral checklist but by looking out for our neighbors, especially the ones who have been denied opportunities to enjoy their basic dignity.

The specific details come later, not here in this passage. Readers of Luke will eventually see the ways that Jesus situates himself among those who lack resources and reputations. This is the Gospel in which Jesus embraces an apparent villain executed alongside him, in response only to an unvarnished request for mercy (Luke 23:42-43). Maybe John cannot yet fully make out exactly what the Messiah will do or what his baptism "with the Holy Spirit and fire" will make possible. John seems to have grasped, though, that what's coming certainly won't end up leaving the world worse for future generations. On the contrary, it's going to be magnificent and hard to miss, for in the end "all flesh shall see the salvation of God."

John 1:6-8, 19-34

If you've read your way through the Gospels, you've likely noticed how different John is compared to the other three, in terms of its structure, vocabulary, and symbolism. That's not a problem crying out for a solution. We read John best if we let it speak for itself and tell its story of Jesus with its own integrity instead of trying to combine or reconcile it with the others. When it comes to how this Gospel describes the voice of John the Baptist, the focus falls mainly on him identifying Jesus as the Messiah as opposed to guiding people to prepare themselves to meet him.

I have a close friend, another Bible scholar, who will probably scold me for referring to "John the Baptist" in the previous paragraph, when the wider context is an investigation of John's Gospel. That's because this Gospel never refers to John as "John the Baptist." He's just "John." She likes to refer to him, then, when talking about John's Gospel, as "John Not the Baptist." But that's her joke, not mine, so I won't use it anymore. I'll keep referring to him as "John the Baptist" so we don't confuse him with the book that's also called John. The name *John* was popular in the first century. It's a challenge to keep track of them all.

More noteworthy: There is no account of Jesus being baptized in John's Gospel, as he is in the other three. We find plenty of references to John the Baptist performing his ritual in John, but for some reason we never get to observe it happening to Jesus. This is probably a way for John (the Gospel) to reassert Jesus's superiority over John the Baptist. It's Jesus's story, and he needs no authorization from a human being, for he comes directly from God.

At the same time, John the Baptist plays a crucial role in recognizing Jesus in John. The Gospel introduces him as "a witness to testify to the light." The light is Jesus, according to John 1:4-5 (see also John 3:19; 8:12; 9:5; 12:46). John is the first character in the story who knows who Jesus is, explicitly pointing him out as "the Lamb of God," the one in whom the Holy Spirit dwells, and "the Chosen One" or "the Son of God" (depending on which Bible translation you are reading for John 1:34). Because of all the clarity that John the Baptist provides in John, my friend also refers to him as "John the Witness," but I'm still sticking to my plan of using only "John the Baptist."

John's Gospel is not such an outlier that we can't see some parallels between this passage and the other three we have explored. It presents John the Baptist as a forerunner who prepares a "way." It has him declare his subordinate status to Jesus, which takes on a particular aspect because this Gospel introduces Jesus as "the Word" who "was in the beginning with God" and who participated in creation (John 1:1-3, which we will explore in chapter 3). Therefore, John the Baptist says Jesus "was before me." Also, John's Gospel depicts John the Baptist's signature ritual as a rite done to prepare people in some way for the Messiah's coming, although we're told little else about what it means to prepare. John the Baptist's apocalyptic themes do not show up clearly in this Gospel, however, compared to the others. Yet the main difference we see in our current passage lies in the lack of ambiguity in the Gospel of John's presentation of John the Baptist's unmistakable insight into Jesus. If there were still disciples of John the Baptist roaming around when John's Gospel was written at the end of the first century, this story aims to point them to Jesus. If John's ongoing reputation as a courageous spiritual leader still remained strong enough to lend credibility to memories about him, this story leans on John's legacy to call attention to Jesus.

In other words, John the Baptist's voice offers a statement of certainty: We've found our Messiah.

Everything is slightly fuzzier in the other Gospels. Yes, John the Baptist foresees something and someone coming, but Matthew, Mark, and Luke aren't precise about who knows what. When Jesus is an adult getting baptized in those Gospels, and the announcements and wonder of the Christmas stories in Matthew 1–2 and Luke 1–2 have faded from view, everyone in the narratives has to learn who he is. In

45

Mark 1:10-11 no one besides Jesus apparently sees the Holy Spirit or hears a voice from heaven. It's similar but more ambiguous in Luke 3:21-22. In Matthew 3:13-15 John recognizes that there's something strange about him baptizing Jesus, but even then only Jesus sees the Holy Spirit come to him in the following verse. Immediately after these scenes in all those Gospels, Jesus goes to the wilderness where the devil tests him to entice him to cling to counterfeit understandings of how he will exercise his power (Matthew 4:1-11; Mark 1:12-13; Luke 4:1-13).

In John's Gospel, John the Baptist reports that he previously witnessed the Holy Spirit come to Jesus and received confirmation from God. This Gospel also includes no account of Jesus being tested in the wilderness. John the Baptist knows who Jesus is. Jesus himself understands who he is and what he has come to do. *Let's get rolling, then*, John's Gospel asserts.

Don't settle for simply noticing that John the Baptist bears witness to Jesus. Consider, too, that his witness refers to Jesus as "the Lamb of God who takes away the sin of the world." No other Gospel uses that title for Jesus. It refers primarily to the Gospel of John's depiction of the Crucifixion, in which Jesus is killed in the hours before the arrival of the first day of Passover, starting at sunset. John likens Jesus to a lamb killed just before Passover begins as part of the liberation God provides for Hebrews enslaved in Egypt (Exodus 12). A Passover lamb was not considered a payment or a sacrifice for sin but a means by which God claims God's people and rescues them from oppression. John the Baptist goes beyond proclaiming the arrival of a nondescript deliverer, then; he implies that Jesus is going to obliterate anything that keeps us from experiencing life in its fullness. At Advent and Christmas, we rightly sing about more than the birth of a baby and a generic sense of hope. Our testimony, like John's, is more specific.

As the hymn "Come, Thou Long-Expected Jesus" declares, Jesus is "born a child and yet a king," specifically one "born to set thy [God's] people free."[4]

Speaking of hymns, the first verse of "What Child Is This" reminds me a little bit of John's John the Baptist too. The hymn begins with a question that anyone unfamiliar with Christmas might easily ask; it's essentially, "What's the big deal with this baby?" Midway through the first stanza the choir or congregation bears witness, like John the Baptist: "This, this is Christ the King!"[5] At that lyric, we should all be pointing our index fingers at Jesus. In John's Gospel, John the Baptist *knows* who Jesus is. He *identifies* who Jesus is. He *directs others* to recognize Jesus too. Older translations read, "Behold the Lamb of God" instead of, "Here is the Lamb of God." "Behold" means "Look!" or "Pay attention!" John the Baptist wants everyone to know: The arrival of this person changes everything.

John's Gospel places great value on correctly recognizing who Jesus is, for to recognize him is to know him and to know the God who sent him (for example, John 4:29; 9:35-38; 10:4, 14; 12:20-21; 14:9; 17:20-21; 20:16, 29). When we read about John the Baptist announcing Jesus's identity to others, we can feel a sense of reassurance that we are part of a long lineage of witnesses who have come to know Jesus Christ and can recognize him among us. When we absorb John's testimony, and when we repeat it ourselves during Advent, we can know that God remains faithful to us, determined to set us free.

MATTHEW 11:2-11

John the Baptist gets only a limited amount of time on the narrative stage in all four Gospels. After all, Jesus is the main attraction, and so John is important to these books only insofar as he informs us, their readers, about Jesus.

In all the scenes we've explored so far, John comes across as rather confident. That changes in this scene, because we detect confusion, impatience, or maybe even doubt. It's understandable, for John has been incarcerated since authorities apprehended him in Matthew 4:12. Evidently John's arrest provokes Jesus, because immediately after it happens, Jesus moves to a new town and starts preaching in public. Maybe the persecution unleashed on John becomes the last straw for Jesus, making the fire in his own bones too hot to hold inside. Eventually Herod Antipas will order John to be beheaded (Matthew 14:1-12). The current scene in Matthew 11 (along with a parallel account in Luke 7:18-35) provides us our only biblical glimpse of John between his arrest and execution.

Matthew does not say explicitly that incarceration demoralizes John. I can see how it might, though. John yearned for God to turn the world right side up, but instead he finds himself held captive according to the same tired script, in which powerful people get their way and manage to squelch a voice calling for justice.

John sends his question to Jesus—"Are you the one who is to come, or are we to wait for another?"—*after* learning about Jesus's recent activities. It's hard to imagine he's upset with what Jesus is doing, but where's the winnowing that John envisioned? What's really changed in the world? Why are the Herods and their ilk still keeping their grip on power?

Jesus does not produce a smug reply. He merely lists ways he has started turning the world around, one person and one illness at a time. Jesus isn't confronting the systems and the power brokers head-on as much as he's showing up for the people whose names no one seems to know. Jesus's ministry might not be playing out precisely as John hoped and anticipated, especially with regard to its scale and immediacy. Yet it seems Jesus is still conducting a reckoning of sorts.

He might not be actively ridding the world of its petty tyrants but he is targeting other things that cause misery. He's erasing the boundaries that we might have wrongly presumed are in place to separate the privileged from the pitied or the healthy from the sick. He's showing that no ailment, no suffering, and even no death is so strong and repellent that divine holiness cannot reach it and transform it.

In addition, and so we don't carelessly overlook it, note that Jesus also praises John for his faith and commitment. There is no scolding here. It's acceptable to have questions and to wonder sometimes if Jesus even knows what he's doing.

There are Advent lessons in this story of John's ruminations about what kind of Messiah God has apparently sent. For one thing, the incongruity John experiences between his expectations and the body of work that Jesus is producing highlights the ways that the Christmas story confounds many of our usual categories. In other words, we might not get the Messiah we expect. We might want God to act with brute strength or God to launch a movement that wields the authority to claim (or to hijack) our cultures and governments for Jesus Christ. But we get a baby born in a manger to parents in risky circumstances, to say nothing of a crucifixion as a grand and ironic display of his "power." We might want a God who gives us perfect moral superiority and vindication, but we get a Messiah who tells us to love our enemies and to pray for those who oppress us (Matthew 5:44; Luke 6:27). We have to sit at the manger in stunned silence for a while and eventually journey to the cross and empty tomb before we can make any firm conclusions. It's Advent, so things are still unfolding; get ready to be amazed.

Also, John reminds us that it's very difficult to live on the brink. I mean, it's not easy to live on the edge of something that you can perceive but can't quite step into. John knows the promises God has made in the past. He's ready for God to fulfill them. But he still dwells on the cusp of fulfillment, longing for it to begin. Patience easily wears thin on the brink.

As I said in chapter 1, Christianity is an Advent religion. Our faith carries within it a sense of "in-betweenness" that also characterizes the season of Advent. Promise and fulfillment don't exactly touch each other, at least not as solidly as we might wish. Promises cultivate patience in us. At the same time, a desire for fulfillment fuels a sense of urgency. We've read the Gospels, and we've considered Jesus Christ, so we believe that this reality called "the kingdom of God" is a game-changer. Nevertheless, we know—because we read the news and talk with our neighbors—that the Kingdom isn't fully here yet. Through it all we trust that Jesus is on the job, sometimes in ways we haven't thought to imagine yet, as well as in ways we haven't imagined to think about yet.

In Conclusion

We need John's voice in Advent. John identifies Jesus for us. He is the first human being to do so when Jesus is an adult. (In chapters 3 and 4 we will see other people who discover who Jesus is, both before and at his birth.) As the Gospels tell their stories, John is also vital for setting Jesus into a context of agitation and protest. John expresses dissatisfaction with the current state of affairs. He's eager for God to inject new life and forgotten convictions into the world. John leads us to reflect on our own expectations and frustrations. John urges us to get ready.

But there's more. John's voice is also a visionary voice. I've mentioned that John is far from "normal" in his ancient cultural terrain. Visionaries, in any society, often come across as a little odd, because they see the world differently. They see possibility differently. Some of them see the ways that innocent people are made to suffer because of how the world is. Some of them have a knack for seeing through the lies our societies tell themselves. Visionaries don't just diagnose problems, they see a new future within reach.

I admit I get flustered when I hear Christians talk about Advent purely as a season of contemplation. People say, "Slow down, don't get caught up in the rush!" I understand their point, but I also think, "Try telling that to John the Baptist!" You might hear a contradiction in these stories about John or perhaps in the way I'm describing the Bible's insights into Advent. I prefer to see it as a tension, a balancing act, instead of a contradiction. In a tension, both aspects pull on each other and influence each other. On one side, John the visionary gives voice to expectations that can agitate us and make us eager to spring into action. More accurately, we beseech God to spring into action and fix what's wrong. On the other side, Jesus, especially in the message he sends back to answer John's questions, reminds us that we follow *him* and stay attentive to where and how he leads. He's changing the world, but it's his road that we're walking on the way to restoration. Moreover, the road can't skirt the cross ahead.

In the tension I've described and in the range of emotions we hear in John's voice, let these biblical passages stir an Advent imagination. Remember our focus on active hope. Advent is a season of restless waiting. Christians might appear to be a little out of step with their neighbors who are rushing to get to Christmas by making it a holiday that begins as soon as December starts (or sooner!). That's not because Christians are preaching "Patience is a virtue!"

It's because we need a little time to imagine. After all, we've been instructed to expect big things.

CHAPTER 3

THE VOICES OF MARY, ZECHARIAH, AND THE GOSPEL OF JOHN

Clarifying New Discoveries with Old Insights

Passages We Will Explore:

- Luke 1:26-80
- John 1:1-18

It happened to me so frequently when my children were growing up. Something they said or did would get me to respond, and as soon as the words were out of my mouth I knew it: I sound just like my mother or father. It didn't matter how much I tried to cultivate my own parenting style or think on my own terms. Sometimes a situation would unfold and it was like I was instinctively thrown back in time, except now I was in a different role. I assume you have had similar experiences.

Even though we may cringe when they happen, something about those moments reminds us—whether painfully, joyfully, or somewhere in between—that we come from somewhere. Our outlooks are all influenced to some degree by the codes and norms that others taught us. Our perspectives on our lives and our world may change, but it's often striking to notice the ingrained vocabulary, adages, and values that we draw from to make sense of our experiences and bring a sense of order to our existence. And I smile because I know someday future generations will be stuck with my voice somewhere in the back of their heads, whether they like it or not.

As the author William Faulkner famously wrote in his novel *Requiem for a Nun*, "The past is never dead. It's not even past."

The coming of Christ provokes a response. In Luke's Gospel, the account of Jesus's birth quickly morphs into a narrative about angels singing, *"Gloria in excelsis Deo"* (Latin for "Glory to God in the highest," quoting Luke 2:14). In Matthew's Gospel, Jesus's arrival causes magi (magicians or priests) from a country to the east to undertake a journey to offer precious tribute to the newborn king. It also makes a tyrannical monarch so scared and hostile that he goes to horrific lengths to try to kill the child (Matthew 2). People—and angels—are trying to make sense of what's happening and what this birth means. They draw on and reproduce hopes and fears etched deeply within the history of God's interactions with the creation.

In this chapter we will consider ways in which two Gospels express the significance of Jesus's arrival two thousand years ago. The voices that speak at the beginnings of Luke and John tell us that Christmas is about the birth of a child unlike any other. As those voices focus on what's new and wonderful about that child, the Messiah, nonetheless they do not allow us to lose track of the past. In them we hear echoes of older voices. We learn that Luke and John display insights that have been inherited from stories and teachings that came before them and were passed along through generations. Those old scripts and

wisdom help these Gospels declare what we can expect to discover—
or rediscover—about God at Christmastime. As a result, our Advent
imagination expands, making space for mysteries and expectations
too far-reaching to fit in a manger alone.

DO YOU HEAR WHAT I HEAR?

When Luke and John speak about who Jesus is and where he comes
from, they're doing theology. People commonly have the wrong idea
about theology. Even the word *theology* has a way of evoking visions
of rooms filled with dusty books or convents and monasteries where
people pray ten hours a day. I think we should imagine theology as
something less complicated and more accessible. A friend once shared
with me the best definition of theology I've ever heard, because it's
accurate, short, and sweet: *Theology is talk about God.*

Often people are prompted to do theology—that is, to talk about
God—when they are feeling reflective, when they meet someone with
very different views, or when their circumstances become especially
difficult or surprising. In other words, sometimes the routines of life
and the things we do to keep us busy or distracted hit a speed bump,
leaving us wondering what's going on, why something is happening,
or what it's all supposed to mean. If your wonder ever leads you to
consider things beyond what you can see or handle, you might be
doing theology yourself.

The Bible includes many stories in which something dramatic
or inexplicable occurs and a person steps up with an interpretation.
Because it's the Bible we're talking about, you won't be surprised
that those interpretations usually have to do with questions about
whether God might be involved in what's happening. For example,
after the enslaved Hebrews safely get across the Red Sea and spot the

Egyptian army dead on the seashore, Moses's sister Miriam grabs her tambourine (apparently she was confident enough to pack one for her hurried escape from Egypt) and sings a song that credits God for their amazing escape (Exodus 15:20-21). Later on, numerous prophets and authors in the Old Testament reckon with the question of why God might permit the Babylonians to overrun Jerusalem and send many of the humiliated residents of ancient Judah into exile in 586 BCE. In the New Testament, when the apostle Peter addresses a large crowd on Pentecost to explain the day's incredible events, he answers the question, "What does this mean?" by claiming God is fulfilling a promise made centuries previously (Acts 2:5-16). Often the Bible presents these kinds of pronouncements through speeches people give, in songs (or psalms) they sing, or by describing object lessons that involve a prophet acting out symbolic messages.

As we will see in the passages we're about to explore, sometimes the Bible offers its interpretations of new experiences by using old ideas and repeating or refashioning them for new circumstances. Well-tested convictions, memories of past experiences, or themes woven through existing documents are often the raw materials out of which new "talk about God" arises. Sometimes an ancestor's voice continues to reverberate.

Old ideas can expand in new settings and take on additional meanings. Old ideas can be true in more than one way.

I left hints about this in chapter 2, when I mentioned that Mark introduces John the Baptist with a combination of phrases and imagery from several Old Testament passages (Mark 1:2-3). Artists would call what Mark is doing a pastiche. Rock, pop, blues, and hip hop musicians would compare it to sampling. Old tunes and ideas are expressing something new. Mark can draw from Isaiah 40:3 to characterize John's work as an effort to transform paths in the wilderness into straight roads. That does not mean that Isaiah 40:3 wasn't also communicating something in its original context over five centuries earlier, when the prophet used the same imagery to describe a joyful return to Jerusalem from exile in a foreign land. Connecting John the Baptist to that original description of restoration after an exile adds a sense of familiarity to John's activity. God is up to something again, and it resembles things God has done before.

A similar dynamic is operating in one of the scenes from Luke that we'll consider in this chapter. When Mary offers her interpretation of the significance of what is happening to, around, and in her during her pregnancy (Luke 1:46-55), her poetry resembles another biblical mother's statement of praise. Hannah, the mother of the prophet Samuel, also extols God's goodness and power soon after her child is born as a result of an extraordinary conception (1 Samuel 1:1-20). Hannah's prayer in 1 Samuel 2:1-10 evidently served as a model for Mary's interpretation of what is afoot in the coming of Jesus.

Paying attention to the connections and echoes in Scripture matters for our knowledge of how biblical stories were composed, but more important is the insight that Scripture is frequently in conversation with itself. The Bible can re-endorse previously made claims about God or reshape them. It accentuates ways in which old ideas accumulate new meaning through new experiences.

The authors who wrote the Gospels could have composed stories to depict the coming of Jesus as something entirely unprecedented or even the work of a new or different deity. Yet they emphatically did not do so. They regularly keep their memories of Jesus tethered to the Old Testament. As the Gospels talk about God and the arrival of Jesus as a manifestation of God's intentions, they remind us that nothing is entirely new. Sure, surprises occur and our expectations are often corrected. The amazement of Jesus's birth and the early church's conviction that the Messiah is God's own Son and God's own self nevertheless resulted in Gospels that anchor those new developments in an old and continuing story. The story began long before Mary and even Hannah came along.

In a sense, we do something similar every Advent. In the pages of Scripture, as well as in our music, symbols, and prayers, we recall voices from the past to help us say something about our present and about the future we desire. Like the people and angels in the Bible, we need something to say at Christmas too. We need to consider what all of this means for us. The opening chapters of both Luke and John take us back to the first century and earlier, but we don't consult those passages merely out of a sense of nostalgia or as an exercise of strengthening our memory. We read and reread them to realize how we, too, inherit insights and old, reliable scripts that help us discover something new—new, at least, to us—in the familiar story of Christmas. That's part of what it means for us to expect that Jesus somehow still arrives among us again and again.

In Luke 1 and John 1 we have before us some of the Bible's most exquisite poetry. It urges us to see the coming of Jesus on a massive, even cosmic, scale. Before we encounter the baby born in Bethlehem, these voices direct our attention to the whole world and to all creation. Nourishing our hopes with their familiar convictions about God, the voices give us a sense of the magnificence of God's promises to love and mend the world.

LUKE 1:26-80

Do you have a favorite part of the Bible? Maybe a verse, a passage, a book, an event, or a character? For me, it's the first two chapters of Luke. Maybe that's no surprise, considering I wrote a book about Advent.

There's something satisfyingly understated about Luke 1–2. Yes, these chapters involve earth-shattering things: The birth of the Messiah and angelic visits are not exactly ordinary events. Yet they also introduce us to people who might have been easy to overlook if you were walking through villages in the first century. We meet Elizabeth and Zechariah, a childless couple evidently old enough to be beyond any possibility of conceiving. Mary, from a small town in Galilee, is an unwed mother-to-be. Unnamed shepherds show up; they could be a little funky. Then there are Simeon and Anna, who both appear to be old and unneeded anywhere else in the world except in the Temple. Not a celebrity in sight.

Nevertheless, all of them have access to remarkable truths about what's going on. They know the story unspooling in front of them is about more than surprising pregnancies and babies. The hope of the world hangs in the balance. Salvation is showing itself. Or, as the hymn "Love Has Come" puts it:

> Love has come and never will leave us!
> Love is life everlasting and free.
> Love is Jesus within and among us.
> Love is the peace our hearts are seeking.[1]

The people in these chapters use their insights about love, life, and peace to instruct us about how to perceive Jesus.

When I teach Luke to seminary students who have already taken an introductory Greek course, I have to be sure they aren't discouraged by what they encounter in Luke 1–2. They might be excited to put their newly acquired language skills to work, but they quickly discover that the syntax of these chapters is not what they thought it would be. They learned to read the style of Greek that was in popular use during the first century, which helps them with the New Testament as a whole, but Luke does something clever in these chapters. The Gospel uses an older style, one that employs a syntax that was more common about two centuries prior to Jesus and that is therefore unfamiliar to my students. Why use Greek from that period? Because that's when Jewish Scriptures (essentially, what Christians eventually came to call the Old Testament) were translated from Hebrew to Greek, because most Jews then were speaking Greek. (The name of those translations is the Septuagint.)

Luke is imitating the style of Jewish Scripture that was still being read and heard when this Gospel was written. Imagine if I suddenly slipped into English from the King James Version. Thou wouldest notice. Luke especially imitates the style found in narrative portions of the Old Testament. The imitation sets the tone for what is happening, then, implying that the story of Jesus continues a long-running history. Luke's narrative sprouts more or less organically within a garden full of older stories about God. The good news about Jesus encompasses a lot of time, land, and people—both in the past before the first Christmas and in the future to come beyond the first Easter.

Prior to the passage we are about to explore, we learn from an angel named Gabriel that Elizabeth will conceive a son who will be named John. This is the story of John the Baptist's origins. Zechariah can't believe it's possible, so Gabriel strikes him mute, possibly to avoid a prolonged argument with him. The angel has no time to deal with a man seeking definitive evidence about what's happening in his wife's womb. As Luke continues, Elizabeth keeps on talking, however, and she interprets her pregnancy as a token of God's favor toward her.

Then we reach verse 26, which begins the scene that Christian tradition remembers as "the Annunciation." It inspired the hymn

"The Angel Gabriel from Heaven Came" and countless pieces of visual art that try to capture a sense of the extraordinary breaking into the life of an otherwise ordinary young woman. Gabriel visits Mary and informs her that she has "found favor with God" and will conceive, carry, and give birth to "the Son of the Most High," who will reign forever. Mary, unsurprisingly, has questions. Gabriel reassures her that the pregnancy will result from the Holy Spirit and "the power of the Most High." Gabriel's announcement concludes with a sentence that encapsulates the whole message of Advent and Christmas well: "Nothing will be impossible with God." (A similar statement—really, a rhetorical question—appears in another biblical story about an unlikely pregnancy, in Genesis 18:14, when Sarah laughs at the prospect of her becoming pregnant. The past is never forgotten.)

Mary, in an understated fashion, offers her consent to the plan: "Here am I, the servant of the Lord; let it be with me according to your word." And everything changes.

Writer and Methodist pastor Jan Richardson composed a marvelous poem about this scene called "Gabriel's Annunciation." It's written in the angel's voice after the event and reflects back from his perspective on Mary and what was about to happen to her and to the world, once he delivered the news. Richardson paints a verbal picture of a nervous angel, overcome by the weight of the moment and what it will mean for Mary, changing her life forever and (assuming you know how the Gospel story will go) exposing her to stigma, risk, and grief. Gabriel finds himself stunned by how the grace-filled Mary "inhabited" both herself and her exchange with him. Finally, Mary's consent speaks grace to the angel, releasing him from the anguish his weighty task lays on him. The poem takes Mary's consent as the story's turning point and a statement of her generosity to all the world. In the succinct last lines of the poem, Gabriel stands in awe of

> her beautiful and
> awful *yes*.[2]

There are many reasons why we should pay attention to Mary's "yes." Biblical stories and the bulk of the Christian tradition—under the supervision of men—have given a lot of attention to Mary's sexual history. By contrast, people rarely ask about Joseph's, and the Bible doesn't talk about it. Some traditions refer to Mary with the term *God-bearer*, which can be heard as reducing Mary's usefulness only to having a womb as opposed to the richer understanding of being a mother, which obviously entails contributions to a child that extend well beyond giving birth. Focusing on Mary's consent is essential. It helps us view her as less of an object and more of a participant, even a collaborator. In our own cultural landscape, it's especially important to interpret this scene as one in which Mary is an active agent and not someone whose body is forced into pregnancy against her will.

The story of Jesus's birth remains a story of divine initiative, but Mary's consent reminds us that human contributions also play a part. The larger narrative of Luke spotlights Jesus's self-giving, but Mary gives too. She has to endure any shame that might come her way as an unwed pregnant woman in a patriarchal culture. She helps equip Jesus for what is to come for him (see Luke 2:51). She accompanies him through his suffering (see Acts 1:14), even as she suffers from it herself (see Luke 2:34-35). Those actions and devotion make Mary highly favored in our estimation, and they also call us to say yes to what God might ask of us.

Mary doesn't have to face her risky future alone. She goes to visit Elizabeth, for they are related to one another (although the Bible never discloses their exact relationship). If Mary did not know about it previously, Gabriel's mention of Elizabeth's pregnancy might have given her strength and courage to step into her newly disrupted life. When angels depart, and majestic experiences fade away into the return of ordinary life, it's good to have an empathetic companion who can help you make sense of what's going on.

At the same time, extraordinary things continue in the scene that churches refer to as "the Visitation." Elizabeth feels her son leap inside her. (Evidently John the Baptist was feisty and intense from before birth!) The Holy Spirit fills her, and she praises Mary for her role in what is unfolding.

Mary responds with a speech in which she interprets what's happening as an act of God, one in line with other acts of God. She speaks as a prophet, for she describes who this emerging story of the Messiah within her is about and explains where it is headed. The speech is sometimes called a canticle or a song. It's also a prayer. Traditionally it is known as the Magnificat, for that is the first word in the Latin translation of the song. It has inspired numerous musical pieces, including traditional sacred works like Bach's "Magnificat," modern hymns like "Canticle of the Turning (My Soul Cries Out with a Joyful Shout)," and rock and roll like "Magnificent" by U2.

As you'll recall, the song imitates Hannah's prayer from 1 Samuel, so Mary reminds us of other people's experiences with God within a more extensive scriptural tableau. In addition, the majority of clauses that come from Mary's mouth resonate with passages or images from the Old Testament. There are too many to list. Mary isn't spouting innovative ideas here, she's drawing from a rich tradition to describe the new happenings around and within her.

The song begins with Mary talking about her own place in everything: *Her* soul "magnifies" and "rejoices" in God, who has "looked with favor on" *her*. The story that her song tells about God begins in her own experience. She doesn't describe God for the sake of creating definitions or doctrine. This isn't that kind of theology. Mary describes God, first, by asserting what she knows in herself to be true about God. She adds her name to the long list of people who have something to say about the mercy of the God of Israel.

God's goodness is not limited to her or to others who have had unusual experiences. Her song is not about elevating elite, special spiritual experiences above all others, for divine mercy goes out to all "who fear" God, "from generation to generation."

In the second half of the song (Luke 1:51-55), Mary makes a series of declarations about God and what God tends to do. A number of vigorous verbs indicate decisive actions. For example, God "has shown strength" and "has scattered the proud." The past tense of those verbs might prompt us to scour the Old Testament in search of what specific events Mary has in mind, but that would misread what she's saying. Instead of reciting God's résumé of discrete accomplishments, Mary offers a character sketch. She's summarizing, not cataloging. What she names are the kinds of things God does and the kinds of promises God regularly makes. The implication is that God is at it again, acting dramatically now in Mary's pregnancy and all that it will eventually make possible. Whatever she perceives about the future her son will bring about, it looks familiar to her, given what she and her ancestors already have learned about God.

Several of the actions we read about describe a reversal of the usual state of affairs. God brings *down* the people who are powerful and lifts *up* those with a lowly profile. God feeds people who are hungry and dismisses those who are wealthy. Jesus will describe a similarly inverted social order later in his ministry (Luke 6:20-26; 18:24-25). I noted in chapter 1 that there are subversive undertones running through Advent. Mary makes them louder. She asks us to look at what her son will do in the coming narrative as more than an impressive display of kindness and charity. He's out to reorder the values, privileges, and blessings that societies use to protect some people's power and comfort while they consign other people to "lesser" status. God's love and justice can upset all of our calibrated measures of who matters and who doesn't. No wonder powerful people will want to kill Jesus as this story rolls on.

Remember the Dietrich Bonhoeffer sermon I described in the introduction? Mary has a similar sense of the magnitude of the power about to be unleashed in the world. God loves the world too much to let its characteristic injustices continue. Jesus of course won't seize political office and legislate or tyrannize his way into creating a just society. Mary's song nevertheless invites us to consider how his coming reiterates God's commitment to see justice water and sustain the world. She's clear that God is the one who makes it happen. The song is about God, not a political party or a list of economic policies we might want to ascribe to God.

From the Magnificat, then, we can infer that Mary's interpretation of what's going on involves something quite more comprehensive than the arrival of an era of good vibes and the promise of paradise after we die. The arrival of the Christ means change, but it's change that God has been talking about and working toward already for a long time.

Mary reminds me that God's commitment to humanity's well-being is something we have to talk about and look for, otherwise it just becomes some article of faith that we store in a closet and never notice. We have to remind ourselves. We have to remember and reassert what people who have gone before us have claimed about God's grace. We have to recall the messages of other poets and prophets. We have to find our place in that grace and embrace what Mary sings about: The salvation of God and its vision for a new way of living is available and active now. We have to enlist ourselves in what's already underway, like Mary does.

Three months pass and Elizabeth gives birth. No one takes her seriously when she wants to name her son John, but when Zechariah miraculously regains his speaking ability, people seem fine with the idea. In fact, they're scared by what is happening and presume that this newborn John must be headed for greatness. Zechariah then offers a speech, in part to direct folks' attention away from John and toward another child who is about to be born, although Zechariah never identifies Jesus by name.

Luke introduces the speech as an act of prophecy. It, like the Magnificat, collects and knits together a number of allusions to the Old Testament. Zechariah, very much a product of his Jewish identity and upbringing, draws on old insights he has been taught to give an account of a new development. Also like the Magnificat, this speech has a lyrical quality and so can be considered another canticle or prayer. You may know it as the Benedictus, which is the Latin translation of its opening word, "Blessed." It likewise has been adapted into many pieces of liturgical music.

Because we know where the narrative is headed, we realize that Zechariah begins by referring to Jesus, not John, as "a mighty savior." That expression comes from a Greek expression that means, literally, "a horn of salvation." (The "horn" in question is the kind on an animal's head, which the Bible takes as a sign of strength. It's not a horn like a tuba, which in our era is a sign that you're going to need a minivan if your child shows interest in playing one.)

Zechariah makes it clear that the arrival of this savior is a fulfillment of expectations from the Old Testament, such as a new king from the lineage of David (see, for example, 2 Samuel 7:12-13, 16), a form of divine protection (a frequent theme in the prophetic books), and a tangible recognition that the covenant God made with Abraham continues (beginning in Genesis 12:1-3). Zechariah shows his awareness of the larger story that is moving forward here. It's a story about a God who keeps showing up to redeem and deliver.

In verse 76, the song turns its attention to Zechariah's son, John. It identifies him as the one who prepares the road (recall the exploration of Luke 3:1-18 in chapter 2). All the attention given to John in Luke 1 amplifies his importance, but Luke is also careful to emphasize his subordinate status to Jesus.

For the purposes of our study of Advent, the song's final lines deserve special attention. Zechariah describes God's compassion as the impulse behind Jesus's and John's arrivals. Salvation doesn't come because God grudgingly has to make good on a deal. God acts with compassion toward the creation. Zechariah's conviction that "the dawn from on high will break upon us" is a beautiful statement, yet it offers a rendering of a Greek clause that is difficult to translate because it includes a couple of words that have multiple meanings. In other words, the final lines evoke even more than a single translation can capture. For one thing, Zechariah conveys a sense that what's happening is a *visitation*. The word for that appears also at the beginning of the Benedictus, where the song praises God for "look[ing] favorably on" God's people (verse 68). Nothing about this implies a passive God. Recall chapter 1 and the apocalyptic notion that the division between heaven and earth becomes permeable when God chooses to "visit," meaning to act among us and for our behalf.

The Benedictus also speaks of light piercing the shadows ("darkness") to illuminate a way toward peace. Peace is the destination in Luke (see, for example, Luke 2:14; 10:5; 19:38, 42; 24:36), although Jesus must go through strife to get there. In Advent we acknowledge God's resolute commitment to create peace and commit ourselves to be beacons for peace, even through the simple gesture of lighting candles around a wreath as the nights grow longer, in the Northern Hemisphere at least. No matter how thick the nighttime may grow, we proclaim a commitment to walking in "the way of peace."

Advent sets us on that course, as we take our bearings from Mary and Zechariah, with the help of voices from further in the past who have also cried out for the peace that God promises to establish.

JOHN 1:1-18

Few things are more delightfully chaotic than Christmas pageants acted out by children dressed as shepherds, magi, innkeepers, and livestock. Those characters come from the Gospels of Matthew and Luke, as we'll see in chapter 4. I wonder if a children's ministry director somewhere has ever tried to put together a pageant based solely on John's Gospel. You'd need a lot of lasers, neon glow sticks, and elaborate costumes for people to portray the Horsehead Nebula and the Andromeda Galaxy. You'd probably get called into the senior pastor's office on the Monday morning after the show.

As you know from chapter 2, John is the outlier among the four Gospels; it offers its account about Jesus with distinctive vocabulary, themes, and perspective. It has no birth narrative, but it has a lot to say about Jesus's origins and identity. If you want to know about all of that, John says, don't travel back to Nazareth and Bethlehem. Instead, revisit the opening chapter of Genesis and its account of the creation of all things. John situates Jesus within a truly cosmic landscape.

The church has traditionally credited the apostle John, one of the sons of Zebedee (see Mark 1:19), as the author of this Gospel. We have no way of confirming or denying that with anything close to certainty. Whoever wrote it—and it might have been multiple people

The Voices of Mary, Zechariah, and the Gospel of John

or someone benefitting from the memories and perceptions of many others—had a flair for poetry and the glorious. The way that this Gospel reflects on the significance and mystery of Jesus suggests that it came about as the consequence of a lot of reflection, discussion, and wonder.

The voice that speaks to us from John's Prologue, the first eighteen verses, is the narrator's. Worrying about exactly who wrote it might miss the point. It's better to read and hear that voice simply as one possessing secrets to divulge and a tradition to pass along. Imagine you're watching a film and hearing a voiceover by an actor who speaks confidently and compellingly, as if they're trustworthy, while also with a hint of amazement, as if they have digested the enormity of what they're saying.

As I mentioned, John makes connections with Genesis 1. Read the first five verses of both books and notice how both talk about beginnings, creative activity, speech (or "the Word"), light, and darkness. Even more, John asserts that "all things came into being through" the Word—this Word that both "was with God" and "was God."

John is talking about Jesus as "the Word." We'll soon look more deeply at that term and what it means for understanding Jesus's relationship to God (and his identity as God). At this point, notice the claim that he has been around a long time, since the beginning.

There are other ways that John's Gospel reflects the influence of other texts and ideas in how the Prologue speaks about Jesus. Like me instinctively imitating my parents and like Mary's and Zechariah's songs drawing from the deep well of scriptural claims about God, John shows the influence of older scripts.

Maybe most noteworthy are the scripts about divine wisdom, which had been a part of Jewish religious understanding for centuries prior to Jesus. Closer to the time John was written, probably within a century and a half prior, a book called the Wisdom of Solomon was composed by a Jewish author in Alexandria, Egypt. Although this book is not formally part of Protestant or Jewish Bibles, it is in the Bibles of most Orthodox churches and the Roman Catholic church. In a prayer addressed to God, the book says this about wisdom:

> *With you is wisdom, she who knows your works*
> *and was present when you made the world;*
> *she understands what is pleasing in your sight*
> *and what is right according to your commandments.*
> *Send her forth from the holy heavens,*
> *and from the throne of your glory send her,*
> *that she may labor at my side*
> *and that I may learn what is pleasing to you.*
> *Wisdom of Solomon 9:9-10*

The prayer says God had company when creating the universe, and it asks God to send that same wisdom (personified as a woman, as wisdom is in much Jewish literature) from God's heavenly presence to earth.

I'm generalizing here, but ancient writers (including some whose works are included in all Christian and Jewish Bibles) describe divine wisdom as something like an emanation from God. I like how Wisdom of Solomon 7:26 puts it: "She is a reflection of eternal light, / a spotless mirror of the working of God, / and an image of his goodness."

The wisdom they're referring to is more than cleverness or prudence. It (or she) is an aspect of God that doesn't remain confined to God but can be considered separately, as if divinity itself enlivens or resides within everything that exists. Wisdom expresses God's delight in creation and always has done so (see Proverbs 8:22-31).

People who wrote about wisdom were eager to remind everyone that you can meet God in places other than temple-based rituals or other structured ceremonies. God's presence and blessing imbue all the ordinary aspects of life and are as close to us as the air we breathe.

As I write I'm singing to myself a verse from the old hymn "O Come, O Come, Emmanuel" that appeals to Wisdom (with a capital *W*, to reflect personification, like with "the Word" in John). Notice the reference to Wisdom as a power and presence woven into the fabric of the universe:

> O come, thou Wisdom from on high,
> who orderest all things mightily:
> to us the path of knowledge show;
> and teach us in her ways to go.
> Rejoice! Rejoice! Emmanuel
> shall come to thee, O Israel.[3]

Observe, then, what John is doing in just the first three verses of the Gospel. Very subtly, to tickle the ears of anyone who knows the traditions and can detect echoes, John introduces Jesus as part of God's ongoing creative work and as the very expression of divine fullness. Jesus bears an uncanny resemblance to Wisdom.

Moreover, this Jesus is "the Word." God creates in Genesis 1 by speaking the universe into existence. Divine speech is effective speech, meaning it doesn't just express things; it accomplishes things. A God who sends out words or speech is a God who wants to communicate, a God who wants to be known and be in relationship. Jesus is God's self-description and God's act of connecting to us. Jews and Christians—who both have rich traditions of divine speech and "the word of God"—definitely do not view God as aloof or nonrelational.

The Greek word translated "Word" is *logos*, which has about fifty different meanings if you look it up in a Greek dictionary. It can refer to a word, like what a group of printed letters create. But it also means speech more generally or an act of speaking. The English word *logic* is connected to it, too, for it can imply a sense of reason. Numerous philosophical movements in the time of Jesus considered there to be a kind of grounding principle in the universe, something like a purposefulness or a rational foundation that could provide solid footing for all of humanity's questions about how to live a good or moral life. What did they call that principle? The *logos*.

So that word is doing a lot of heavy lifting in John. Maybe it's fitting, then, that John doesn't give us a treatise about what it means to call Jesus the *Logos*. I tell my students: Ancient writers didn't read dictionaries; they used words. Greek dictionaries are written by scholars many centuries after the fact, as attempts to sort through how ancient people used their words. If you want to know what John means, keep reading. Moreover, in John's Prologue we're encountering something closer to poetry than to philosophical categories. Different ancient audiences might have absorbed that poetry in a range of ways. That's part of its power.

John's Prologue doesn't give us the precise language that church leaders used centuries after this Gospel was written to lay out the doctrine of the Trinity. Let's be content for now that John clearly names Jesus ("the Word") as God while also leaving a distinction between him and God. Similarly, later in John, Jesus will be clearly hailed as God (John 20:28), and he will distinguish between himself and God, whom he calls "Father" (for example, John 17:20-24).

John's practice of using "Father" as a name for God creates problems because it reinforces assumptions that God is male and that masculine associations of parenting (however a culture chooses to define those) are more fitting for describing God than feminine associations are. That's a lot to unpack, especially since I think that we as a society ought to reexamine where those "masculine" or "feminine" associations come from in the first place, how we misuse them, and whom they harm. In any case, God is not male, and the Bible also includes comforting imagery and metaphors for God that are not traditionally masculine, although those tend to attract less attention from New Testament authors than the idea of a divine Father.

It's valid to experience John's repeated use of "Father" as burdensome, if you do. Some people have such terrible impressions of their fathers that the language gets in the way of knowing and trusting God. Similar situations exist for some people and their mothers. At the same time, I'd urge you not to toss out John's parental language entirely, because the parent-child connection that Jesus highlights is a way that John lifts up the deep intimacy that Jesus shares with his heavenly parent. At the core of that intimacy, Jesus promises, is a love that God longs to share with each of us (see John 17:26). According to John 1:12, owing to what Jesus makes possible, anyone else can likewise have that intimacy and belonging as God's child.

The Prologue also brings the cosmic expanse of Jesus and his identity down to earth. Don't think of Jesus the Word as a principle or a kind of abstract projection. How does that help you live your life, anyway? Where the story gets earthy and where it can be said to be a Christmas story, although a very idiosyncratic one that makes it an odd choice for a pageant script, is in verse 14: "And the Word became flesh and lived among us."

John doesn't say the Word became *human* or the Word took on a *body* to take it for a test drive. It's *flesh*. Flesh is what you touch and what touches you when you come into physical contact with someone else. Flesh needs protection from the elements. Flesh can be wounded. It bleeds. It dies.

John refuses to resolve any tension or incongruity we might think exists between divinity and humanity, at least in Jesus, the Word made flesh.

Furthermore, the Greek word translated as "lived" in verse 14 literally means "dwelled in a tent." Again, we are reading poetry and metaphor. Sometimes it's frustrating when translators iron those metaphors out, as though they're afraid readers won't know what to do with them.

The subtle reference to a tent adds a sense of impermanence to Jesus's earthly existence. Later in the Gospel he explains that he must leave and return to "the Father" after his death and resurrection occur (John 14:3, 18-20; 16:28; 20:17). Yet the idea of a tent also implies a sense of hospitality and mutuality that Jesus shares in human community, for it calls to mind dwellings for agricultural laborers and travelers who rely on temporary shelters and cooperation with neighbors to survive.

The fourth verse of "O Come, All Ye Faithful" tries to make sure John's voice gets its share of attention during Advent and Christmas:

> Yea, Lord, we greet thee,
> born this happy morning;
> Jesus, to thee be all glory given;
> Word of the Father,
> now in flesh appearing!
> O come, let us adore him;
> O come, let us adore him;
> O come, let us adore him,
> Christ, the Lord![4]

I would add to the hymn only that our response to John's description of the Word ought to be more than adoration. John presents Jesus as one to be known—not in a purely cognitive or intellectual sense but in a relational one.

There are two additional aspects of the Prologue that I want to highlight, but I trust you can tell that there's even more we could explore. The whole thing is truly a feast. First, notice the connection John draws between the "glory" Jesus possesses and the "grace and truth" he pours out (verses 14 and 16). Glory connotes excellence and power. It might make Jesus come across as intimidating and unapproachable. But this glory manifests itself in grace and truth— gifts that benefit humanity and reveal the generous heart of God. Remember we're talking about a God who becomes better known through Jesus, because Jesus makes himself known in his very self, in his flesh. There's an abundance of grace, "grace upon grace" to experience in Jesus. That's part of what John means in the concluding verse of this passage, which mentions Jesus making God known. We come to know this unseen God through the grace lavished on us by the Son.

John's mention of Jesus's glory does not imply that we have to build a wall around him to protect ourselves. Glory in John is an expression of love. Later in John, in a prayer to God, Jesus says that his glory comes from God, "because you [God] loved me before the foundation of the world" (John 17:24). What does God's love look like, enfleshed? It looks like Jesus.

The second remaining detail comes also from that final verse, which says, "It is the only Son, himself God, who is close to the Father's heart, who has made him known" (1:18). Again, John describes Jesus as God but also distinct from "the Father." More intriguing here, though, is the reference to the intimacy Jesus shares with his "Father." Jesus is very close to God, but it's not so much at the divine "heart" where Jesus resides. It's at the divine *breast*, which is a better way of translating the Greek word in question.

I don't mean to be persnickety about this, and I know that hearts and breasts aren't far apart, anatomically speaking. But the translation matters. "Breast" calls forth a greater sense of intimacy and vulnerability, at least in how I hear it. The relationship Jesus shares with God is not like a solider to an officer or an assistant to a boss. It's like a child pulled in close to share a sense of protection, reassurance, warmth, and love. Even more fascinating: Jesus later declares that he aims to make the same kind of intimacy possible for the rest of us (John 17:26).

What does the coming of Jesus mean? The same power that infuses and animates the entire cosmos with love wants to pull us in tight.

I have to be honest and confess that I don't know what it looks like to *prepare* for that kind of love during Advent. Maybe there's nothing we can do except to accept and treasure the embrace that God provides.

IN CONCLUSION

The three voices we've lingered over in this chapter offer us more poetry than precision. Maybe the songs of Mary and Zechariah and John's Prologue aren't technically poems in terms of their form, but they're all poetic—full of arresting images, wordplay, and imagination. Let's not hurry past that reality too quickly.

So much of the way that Christians, especially American Protestants, understand what it means to engage in "talk about God" (theology) consists of explanation. That makes theology too small and uninteresting. Luke and John might have presented an extended essay to explain what the arrival of the Messiah means for the world, but instead they explore that ground poetically. These books' poetry isn't a shortcut, as if the people who originally put together the Gospels didn't know what they were talking about. I assume they understood that sometimes our "talk about God" is more appropriate when it's poetic. God, I believe, is more like a poem than like a list of facts.

When I teach, especially in congregations, I like to use a projector so I can display art as I speak about the Bible. I'm particularly interested in pieces by artists who create visual representations of biblical stories in styles that are unusually expressive or outside the typical norms of classical medieval art. That's because I want to stir imaginations and remind people that there are different ways of approaching and understanding a biblical passage, partially because all of us as readers come to the Bible from different perspectives. Artists can help us widen our vision and see more expansively. Plus, when the conversation is about God and how God relates to humanity, there are some topics that are either too profound, too far-reaching, or too majestic for conventional theology to capture. Artists and poets can take us to vistas that might be otherwise inaccessible to us. Soak in the view.

What I've just described matters all year long, but Advent offers a particularly appropriate time for us to expand our imaginations. God's visitation and the Word becoming flesh are Advent topics. The fancy name for what we're considering is the Incarnation—the Christian belief that in Jesus (in his embodied self) we encounter divinity and humanity brought together in an inexplicable community and harmony. As we've seen, certain voices from the Gospels tell us that this Incarnation might make us recall other hopes, expectations, and convictions that people have had about God and God's love for the world, but there's also something new afoot in Jesus's arrival. We encounter God in new ways because of the Incarnation. We know

God in new ways, benefit from God in new ways, and find ourselves embraced by God in new ways.

These poetic voices also beckon us to dig deeper and to look a little closer. There's more to talk and sing about during Advent than stories of conception and childbirth.

One of the things I find myself saying occasionally to students is, "The more you know, the more you'll see." Of course, anyone with even a little knowledge about the Bible can still pick it up, read it, and absorb something that usefully informs how they think about God and live in response. I'm not saying that knowing a lot about the Bible makes you a more spiritual or loving person or makes you someone who's always right and gets to lord their knowledge over others. My point instead is: If people learn about the ancient world and its cultures, investigate Jewish teachings from the time of Jesus, study rhetorical conventions that shaped how the New Testament documents communicated to their original audiences, become proficient with biblical Greek and Hebrew, talk with others about what they observe in the Bible, and familiarize themselves with how the Bible has been interpreted over the centuries, they will notice more in the Bible and maybe approach it with a wider imagination. The voices we've just explored would agree. They remind us that we have access to a deep well.

We approach Mary, Zechariah, and John like we do any poet: We listen. Maybe we find ourselves inspired to compose new poems in response. These biblical voices pay attention for signs of the divine around them. They are ready to discover more of them too. As a result, they find truths that give them, and now us, hope.

CHAPTER 4

THE VOICES OF ANGELS AND PROPHETS

Revealing the Messiah

Passages We Will Explore:

- Matthew 1:18-25
- Luke 2:1-38

The birth of Jesus was—and is—an epiphany.

That might sound strange to you if you know that Epiphany is the name of the season that Christians observe after the twelve days of Christmas are complete, beginning on January 6. Technically speaking, January 6 *is* the date for the Feast of the Epiphany, and the rest of the season, up until Lent, is marked as time after *the* Epiphany.

The odd thing is, Christians across the globe have different ideas about what *the* Epiphany is and what they're celebrating. Epiphany means "manifestation," and as a distinctively Christian holiday it remembers Jesus's true self becoming manifest or knowable to the whole world. In other words, the day asks and answers a question: How did the world at large come to know that the Messiah is here?

The reality of the differences of opinion about the day of Epiphany remains unforgettable in my memory. Prior to the COVID-19 pandemic, I was leading a study tour in the Holy Land during

January. We visited Qasr al-Yahud, which is a site along the Jordan River set aside for pilgrims to remember the baptism of Jesus and to wade in the water themselves. Our visit happened to correspond with the day that many Orthodox churches celebrate the Baptism of Jesus, the scene in which Matthew, Mark, and Luke describe the Holy Spirit coming to (or into) Jesus. Not being in the habit of keeping track of Orthodox calendars, I had not foreseen the coincidence. So now I know well: For many Orthodox traditions, Jesus's baptism is *the* day when his identity becomes manifest. And marking the occasion can be quite a party.

Jubilant Orthodox Christians from numerous nations showed up at Qasr al-Yahud in large numbers and on both sides of the river. I was expecting a quiet and reflective opportunity for our group to remember our baptisms, but that was impossible due to how filled the place was. The experience was chaotic, festive, noisy, joyful, and a rather scary, too, because the authorities' crowd-management strategies weren't working and the platform along the river is small. Celebrating the baptism of Jesus isn't exactly a major festival in my Presbyterian congregation each year. For a lot of churches, however, that is *the* epiphany *par excellence*—a day to bear witness to the Messiah's arrival loudly and even with belly flops into the murky Jordan River if that's your thing.

Other traditions associate the day of Epiphany with the visit of the gift-bearing magi (see Matthew 2:1-12). Maybe you or people you know celebrate *Dià de los Reyes* on January 6, honoring the day when notable Gentiles (non-Jews) come from the east to see Jesus and recognize him as a king. In some cultures, that day and not Christmas is the time for exchanging presents.

There are different ways to do Christianity and to honor Jesus, so trust me: I'm not here to start or settle any disagreements about *the* Epiphany when I say that Christmas itself is an epiphany.

The Letter to Titus—one of the more obscure New Testament books that doesn't receive much notice, and usually for good reasons—seconds the motion about Christmas being an epiphany. Titus says, speaking about Jesus, "God's grace became manifest for salvation to all people" (Titus 2:11, my translation). Titus isn't explicitly discussing Jesus's birth, but it characterizes Jesus himself as the *manifestation* of divine grace. Later in Titus, the book's author gives more details about what grace is, speaking of Jesus as a manifestation of God's "goodness and loving kindness" (Titus 3:4). I'd extend these ways of describing Jesus by saying that they apply also to his arrival. The baby born at Christmas is an expression of grace in human flesh, just as Jesus was a walking, breathing epiphany. Divine graciousness is even etched into Jesus through his name, which in Hebrew means "God saves."

Fun fact: in Titus 2:13, the letter describes our waiting for Jesus's future coming as waiting for another "manifestation" of God's glory. Even all the way back to when Titus was written in the early second century CE, we see connections made between Jesus's original arrival and his eventual return. We currently reside in the time between two definitive epiphanies of God's Messiah.

Ancient Greek literature included numerous stories about gods becoming manifest to human beings or somehow manifesting their powers in unobvious ways through human affairs. Those appearances were called epiphanies (*epiphaneiai* in Greek). The original audiences of Titus would know that an epiphany of divine grace is about more than a person having a moment of intellectual insight. Instead, things change when epiphanies occur. Previously unknown truths become apparent. To borrow language from John 1, which we considered in chapter 3, light shines into unlit places. A god makes an appearance.

I'm up to more than wordplay here. To recognize Christmas as an epiphany, an instance of divine revelation, is important, because it might reorient our perspectives on what it means to encounter God. In the introduction I said that Dietrich Bonhoeffer's Advent sermon is on target when it describes the potential terror that could come in response to God appearing among us. A powerful epiphany—a face-to-face with divine holiness—might prompt us to turn our backs, fall to the ground, shield our eyes, or otherwise beg for mercy. But Christmas causes us to reevaluate all of that, because the birth of Jesus, as Matthew and Luke narrate it, is mostly unexceptional. Yes, the conception of Jesus is—well—inconceivable, but when it comes time for Mary to give birth, the Bible remains remarkably understated. No clouds or fire in the room. No earthquakes. Like any other infant, this one must be swaddled (Luke 2:7). The Bible doesn't mention these details, but obviously the baby must be changed and nursed, as well. If you were there, you could hold him or sing him a lullaby.

What an ordinary, extraordinary manifestation of God's presence and saving grace.

It's important to maintain that tension between extraordinary and ordinary as we prepare ourselves for the Christ during Advent. The God of Israel and Jesus Christ becomes known in unexpected situations and to unlikely people across the pages of the Bible. Even now, Jesus continues to show up among those who suffer (see, for example, Matthew 25:31-46). We don't learn about God in only one single way, scene, or verse in the Bible. The same is true for the Gospels' presentations of Jesus's birth.

There are numerous options for how we might examine the Christmas narratives that Matthew and Luke pass along to us. Obviously, the birth itself is the game changer, but we'll see that these Gospels don't say much about labor and delivery. In this chapter we will direct our focus toward the action surrounding that event. When we zoom out from the Nativity scene alone, we'll observe that things get more unusual. We've seen some of that already in the previous chapter, because voices from Luke and John insist that amazing things are in the works at Christmas. Now we will explore the voices in Matthew and Luke that disclose information to other people in the stories: what Joseph learns from a dream about what is happening with Mary, what an army of angels tells and sings to a huddle of frightened shepherds, and what the prophetic insights of two sages named Simeon and Anna reveal about Jesus. Those voices provide insight into Jesus—his names, his purpose, and the road ahead of him. Their insights help us continue to experience and live into an active hope during Advent.

MATTHEW 1:18-25

In the previous chapter I made a bad joke about what a surreal experience it would be to stage a Christmas pageant based solely on the Prologue in John's Gospel. Forgive me for returning to the scene of the crime here while I entertain the thought of a pageant based solely on another Gospel: Matthew. You see, Matthew's version of Jesus's birth, requiring only eight verses, is rather short in comparison to Luke's. It features few characters and little action. No wonder the classic 1965 television special *A Charlie Brown Christmas* has Linus read from Luke 2 instead.

I'm not out to criticize Matthew's version. Each Gospel has its own message to convey, perhaps owing to how its author was aiming to influence the book's original audiences. It's up to us to consider each story and discuss what it has to teach us.

Not much happens in Matthew's account, but what does occur is crucial. Mary gets little attention and comes across as more of an object than an active subject until the final verse, when she gives birth to Jesus. All we learn about her pregnancy is that "she was found to be pregnant from the Holy Spirit," but that leaves a lot of details unspoken. Assuming Mary knows about the Spirit's role, does anyone else? Would anyone believe her if she told them? Instead, the action swirls around Joseph in Matthew, and the major dynamic in the plot is the question of what he should do about Mary. A dream reveals to him what he needs to know, and he acts accordingly.

A pageant about a man having a dream that helps him decide what he should do about a woman in his life is not going to preach well in most churches (thank God). I rest my case about the Matthew-only pageant being a bad idea.

Yes, there is more that happens in Matthew's overall account. You're thinking of the magi who visit with gifts and who appear only in Matthew. But they don't arrive until after Jesus's birth (Matthew 2:1) and apparently up to two years later, according to how the story unfolds (see Matthew 2:7, 16). So most "normal" congregational pageants that include the magi are stretching the timeline. It's understandable. The magi are great roles for aspiring child actors, and they often have the best costumes.

You understand now why Bible scholars are rarely asked to consult on Christmas pageants. We have a way of ruining the fun.

Back to Matthew's account. Don't let the lack of action in these verses distract you from what we do learn from them. Matthew crafts the story as one about God's initiative, God's trustworthiness, and the nature of what it is like to choose obedience in response to God.

At the beginning of the Christmas story, all we know about Joseph is that he is the son of someone named Jacob and will end up being the husband of Mary (1:16). Matthew quickly announces that Joseph is "righteous." Righteous does not mean sanctimonious or too good for everyone else; it means Joseph wants to do the right thing.

Wanting to do the right thing and being courageous enough to do the right thing are one part of the equation. Knowing what the right thing is often proves more difficult, however, and that is where Joseph gets ensnared. Having learned that Mary, his fiancée, is pregnant, he reasons that the right thing is to separate himself from her but as discreetly as possible. He cannot simply end their engagement, as might happen today in some societies. Mary certainly cannot make that decision in their culture. Some kind of legal action was required, perhaps involving negotiations about returning a dowry and releasing the couple from any pledges that might have been made about responsibilities to members of extended families. At least Joseph wants to do it "quietly," which would satisfy the legal obligations while shielding both him and her from excessive public scrutiny. You can almost hear him sighing and saying, "Let's just move on."

Then again, in that outcome, Mary would still be pregnant, and Joseph would not. Easier for him to move on. Matthew doesn't comment on whether Joseph is really acting as righteously as he could, and it's fair for us to be shocked by Mary's lack of participation in the matter. We still have to acknowledge that Joseph has few good or easy options in front of him, at least from his perspective and given the cultural mores around him. We can get detailed if we let deliberations over how virtuous or selfish Joseph might be take over the story. A key point here is that it's a muddled situation, and Mary's unborn child is at risk of being born without a legal father and therefore also without a clear legal line of connection to King David.

We know about the threat to the royal lineage of Mary's child because of the passage that precedes this one. A genealogy at the beginning of the Gospel links Jesus to David through Joseph, not Mary (Matthew 1:1-17). Jewish genealogies at that time were patrilineal (traced through fathers). Only several centuries later did matrilineal descent become more significant for Jewish communities and their sense of ancestry. The genealogies of Jesus's era weren't necessarily based on biology but on legal standing. If Joseph becomes Jesus's father, then in a legal sense Jesus is descended from David. That is part of establishing Jesus's legitimacy as the Messiah who is descended from David. No characters in this Gospel refer to Jesus as the Messiah until Matthew 2:4, but eventually that title and also "Son of David" will be applied to Jesus repeatedly. The irony of all this, of course, is that Jesus is actually God's Son also. Don't ask me to explain that biologically, but it obviously serves as a piece of Matthew's effort to establish Jesus as one with unimpeachable authority.

In a dream an angel tells Joseph how to proceed and explains a little bit about what is happening. Anyone in the audience who knows the Old Testament well might be grinning and nodding. The previously most famous Joseph in the Bible was a dreamer himself. In Genesis 37–50 that Joseph, because of the dreams he had and his ability to interpret other people's dreams, found himself sold into slavery, released from prison in Egypt, installed as a trustworthy adviser to Pharaoh, and eventually positioned to save untold numbers of lives through strategic management of resources during a severe famine. Now in Matthew's Gospel, another Joseph, because of his dreams, helps take the story forward as God wills it. Later, Joseph will respond to an additional dream by leading Mary and Jesus into Egypt to find sanctuary from mortal danger (Matthew 2:13-15). Egypt, where a Pharaoh once caused so much suffering, serves now as a place of refuge.

In the dream, Joseph, addressed by the angel as "son of David" (to remind us of how important Davidic connections are in Matthew), learns how Mary's pregnancy came about and what to name the child who "will save his people from their sins." The angel's voice also instructs him to marry Mary, which he does before Jesus's birth.

Linger over Joseph's obedience for a minute. Originally his worry seems to stem from social pressures, the threat of "disgrace," or broken trust. The angel reveals to Joseph what God has in store, and that is enough to redirect Joseph's attention. He learns what the right thing is for him in this situation, and he does it without hesitation. The angel gives him no token, nothing like a notarized document from God that can prove to other people that everything's fine and in God's hands. All he gets is a promise, which is evidently enough for him.

I don't intend to make it sound easy for Joseph, because it isn't. He has a decision to make when he wakes up, and I imagine that every passing minute of consciousness makes his fading memory of the dream seem crazier. But he decides, choosing to trust the angel's voice.

What a choice—and one made with limited information. If I were the one dreaming, I'd have a frenetic response for the angel: "I want to know more. How will this son save people from sins? How and why is the Holy Spirit causing pregnancies, exactly? How am I supposed to know how to parent a kid who's descended from God?" Not only is Joseph apparently less panicky than I am, he's willing to go forward without knowing much at all about where the story is heading.

That's often what it looks like to choose obedience to God. It involves saying, "I don't know what this road is going to be like or if my journey will be easy or agonizing, but I'm going to walk it." Sometimes we know—or we think we know—the destination where a road will take us, but nonetheless the journey from point A to point B is usually much less clear.

Obedience is a step-by-step affair. For example, I've heard people who understand the work required to do justice much better than I do say things like, "You don't have to have it all figured out before you begin. You don't have to know the solutions. Just take the next best step. It's a long road."

I used to work with an Old Testament scholar who once preached a memorable sermon on Psalm 119:105 ("Your word is a lamp to my feet / and a light to my path"). He explained that lamps in the ancient world were little wicks hanging out of shallow bowls of oil, with each one producing a tiny, flickering flame. If God or Scripture lights our path like that—and not like a modern gas-powered camping lantern shooting 1,000 lumens in every direction—then we shouldn't expect to perceive what's ahead of us in the dead of night by more than a few inches. The psalm says we go one step at a time.

Bound up in our step-by-step obedience is a sense of trust in God, that God will take care of where we are headed. We sometimes need to be careful about how we express that to others, so they don't interpret it as a way of saying something inane, like, "Let go and let God" or, "Whatever happens is God's will." I don't think that obedience to God and trust in God are about facing life with passivity. It takes discernment, discussion, and a willingness to put ourselves out there sometimes to figure out what the next *best* step is.

Joseph has help in figuring it out—divine help. Christmas in Matthew is a story about God's initiative. We're not privy to Mary's participation in what is transpiring. Joseph doesn't have to do much except stick to what he was originally going to do (before learning about his fiancée's pregnancy). Matthew includes no mention of travel or needing to find a place to stay. Jesus is born, and Joseph sees to it that his name is Jesus. By noting that Joseph gives Jesus his name, Matthew indicates that Joseph indeed accepts the child as if he were his own offspring. Jesus belongs to David's family tree. Crisis averted.

As we keep digging into this passage, we discover more evidence of God's initiative. For example, the narrator breaks into the story in verses 22-23 to explain that Mary's pregnancy occurs "to fulfill" something God had previously disclosed through the prophet Isaiah. The Gospel then quotes Isaiah 7:14—not from the original Hebrew version of Isaiah but from a Greek translation found in the Septuagint (which I introduced in chapter 3, while discussing Luke 1:26-80). Matthew reports that God, through Isaiah, once promised that a virgin would become pregnant and bear a son. The implication is that God is now making good on that promise.

If you look up Isaiah 7:14 in your Bible, you'll find a different promise described. There it says, "Look, the young woman is with child and shall bear a son." That's because the translators of modern English Bibles work from the earlier Hebrew version of Isaiah, not the later Greek version that Matthew cites. Why? Because the Hebrew version is the original version, or at least has a much better claim on being a record of what the original version of Isaiah said. (No one has the original manuscripts for any of the biblical writings, in case you were wondering.)

It would take a while and distract us from the task at hand for me to explain all that is going on, historically, behind the creation of discrepancies between the Hebrew and Greek versions and why Matthew cites the Greek version of Isaiah 7:14. I'll leave those explanations to other scholars for now.[1]

The clear differences between Isaiah and Matthew are significant and worth our attention, however. Isaiah speaks of a young woman who is already pregnant and getting ready to bear a child. Matthew speaks of a "virgin" who will at some point in the future conceive a child. Those aren't the same thing. Again, I'll let other scholars guide you through the details of syntax and vocabulary, if you are interested. The point I want to linger over, however, is that Isaiah speaks about something happening in the present tense. The prophet is addressing King Ahaz in the eighth century BCE while Ahaz is scared about an invasion he thinks is imminent. Isaiah sees no threat at this point, so he says to the perturbed king, "Hey!" (I'm paraphrasing, very freely.) "Do you see that pregnant woman over there, across the room? She's going to give her child the name Emmanuel—'God is with us'— because she believes God will preserve us. Her bold trust should give you faith." Matthew, however, following the Septuagint's changes to the passage, rereads Isaiah to make it a statement about a future woman and a future pregnancy in the first century CE.

Don't believe anyone who insists you must make a choice between the original Isaiah 7:14 and the altered Isaiah 7:14 that Matthew republishes. In other words, it's not the case that only one can be *the* correct meaning for all time to the exclusion of the other one. Christians direct too much animosity on a regular basis toward our Jewish neighbors when, among other things, we insist that biblical passages can have only one correct meaning, and we've figured it out. Both groups can legitimately interpret Isaiah differently. It's even possible for us to read multiple meanings out of Isaiah, all while recognizing that the Septuagint makes significant alterations.

In this case, Matthew is not necessarily disputing the significance of what Isaiah said and meant, over seven hundred years prior to Jesus's birth. Matthew should not be taken as a Christian effort to erase the validity of ancient (Jewish) history and Jewish hopes. I'm convinced that we can read this as Matthew *expanding* Isaiah's vision of trust, not diminishing what Isaiah originally proclaimed. The story of an Emmanuel—a sure sign of God's presence and reliability—becomes retold in the story of Jesus. In Jesus, Matthew sees the original promise of a baby emblazoned with hope that "God is with us" restated, made true a second time. That second time is an additional time, transpiring in an additional way, when Mary "is found to be pregnant from the Holy Spirit." Matthew reminds us that stories—especially stories about God's dependability—can be true more than once and true in more than one way. God's faithfulness has a way of looking familiar.

Mostly, I suspect that Matthew really likes the name Emmanuel and is excited to declare it in reference to Jesus, however the name gets there. "God is with us"—what a name.

The name alone is a rebuttal to fear and helplessness. That was established when armies were marching in the vicinity of Jerusalem and drawing King Ahaz's attention. The name speaks defiantly in the face of threats. Whoever the mother was who, according to Isaiah, was going to name her child Emmanuel while vultures were circling knew something about the brazenness of hope. To place the name on a child born into dangerous circumstances is awfully serious and delightfully playful all at once. The meaning of the name is a sentence, and the sentence is a promise.

In Matthew's appeal to Isaiah, the name *Emmanuel* is cast as a promise that God makes. It's a divine pledge not to abandon the world to chaos and destruction.

We don't see it yet in this passage from Matthew, but there's a sense of pending danger implied by referring to another baby as Emmanuel. Matthew will introduce the danger very soon, once the magi appear in Jerusalem and agitate King Herod with their interest in welcoming a newborn king (Matthew 2).

Although Herod's response to the birth of Jesus lies outside of Matthew's Nativity narrative, it serves as a way for this Gospel to illustrate how dangerous Christmas is. Herod interprets the arrival of the Messiah as a threat to his own dominance and a subversion of Roman superiority in general (for Herod rules on Rome's behalf). Herod cherishes power. It's the tool he knows how to use best. He exercises it violently, ordering the death of numerous small children who reside in and around the small village of Bethlehem, hoping one of them is the "king of the Jews" he cannot find (Matthew 2:16-18).

The voice of the angel in Joseph's dream reveals that Mary's child will be a deliverer, a savior. The narrator's voice sums up Jesus's essence with the name Emmanuel. Herod does all he can to prevent any kind of deliverance. If God wants to come near and be with humanity, the temperamental tyrants of this world will do everything they can to resist. They'll go to any lengths in their efforts to crush hope. It's an old story, one often made true again and again through history, unfortunately.

The promise nevertheless endures. In the final sentence of Matthew's Gospel, as the resurrected Jesus addresses his followers for the last time, he says, "I am with you always, to the end of the age" (Matthew 28:20). He remains Emmanuel forever, even though he is physically absent. If we sense that the dangers of Christmas continue in our time, whatever they may be, that promise can give us hope and courage to face what needs to be faced.

LUKE 2:1-38

Joseph is obedient in Luke's birth narrative too. In this account, though, he must obey imperial authorities. That doesn't mean he disobeys God, for Luke never describes God communicating with him. All we know about Joseph from this Gospel is that he is descended from David and engaged to Mary (Luke 1:27; see also 3:23, 31). A census requires him to travel with Mary to Bethlehem, because of his Davidic ancestry. We have no evidence that an empire-wide census took place at this time, and the prospect of making everyone relocate to complete their necessary paperwork (or papyruswork?) is preposterous. Luke isn't telling unvarnished history here as much as calling attention to the Roman Empire's extensive power over people, their movements, and their futures. But not their hopes.

Luke devotes little attention to describing the birth. Artists have filled that gap nicely over the centuries, capturing the beauty, humility, joy, and peril of the scene. Any successful birth is a good birth, for being pregnant in the ancient world (and in some parts of the world still today) was one of the most life-threatening things that could happen to a person.

When we hear a voice for the first time in this passage, it's one with news to reveal. An angel speaks to shepherds in the region around Bethlehem. If you visit in the town of Beit Sahour, in which the traditional site of this event is located, you get a sense of an idyllic scene with gentle, rolling hills.

Of course, we have encountered an angel already in this Gospel, when Gabriel appears to Zechariah and Mary (recall the previous chapter). The word *angel* means "messenger" in Greek. It wasn't a word originally coined to describe heavenly beings, but obviously it has stuck. In a way, the hymn "Hark! The Herald Angels Sing" contains a redundancy, since all angels are, by definition, messengers or heralds. Parts of the Bible describe them as warriors too. That comes to the fore in this scene when Luke refers to "a multitude of the heavenly host," since the word *host* means "army." The Bible on the whole provides very little information about angels. Many common assumptions about angels come from later authors who were influential in shaping Christian understanding. What these angels in the field near Bethlehem look like to the shepherds is anyone's guess, but they appear to be terrifying, for the first words spoken to the shepherds are, "Do not be afraid" (see also Luke 1:12-13, 30).

The angel promises he has "good news" to share. "Good news" and "gospel" are equivalent expressions in English; both come from the same Greek word that appears here. The angel characterizes the announcement of Christmas as a *gospel*, one of "great joy for all the people." Gospel is another word that was already widely used before Jesus came along. In other words, it isn't a uniquely Christian word, although it eventually became closely associated with Jesus, his message, and his followers' message about him. If you lived in a Roman-controlled city in the first century and in the marketplace you heard the buzz that a courier had just arrived and was going to announce a gospel from the emperor, your ears would perk up. It could be propaganda, announcing the latest victories of the Roman army on some frontier, or maybe the emperor's wife just had another son. It might be news you can use, like the declaration of a tax amnesty in your region or a grain giveaway. Let's just say the news was supposed to be *good*, unlike so many of the "breaking news" alerts I see on my phone, which too often ruin my day instead of improving it.

The angel voices remarkable news. The Messiah, a Savior, has just been born in Bethlehem. That's it. That's the news. The angel doesn't mention specifics, like saving people from their sins, as Joseph learns in Matthew 1:21. There's no explicit revelation of exactly where the story is heading next. Return to the hymn "Hark! The Herald Angels Sing." You have to keep reading all of Luke and through the book of Acts to learn what that hymn declares. For example:

> Mild he lays his glory by,
> born that we no more may die,

born to raise us from the earth,
born to give us second birth.[2]

What a great lyric. But the hymn is projecting into the future, which is fine. My point is that the story, as Luke tells it, still contains a great amount of unknowing, which stokes anticipation and curiosity. All the angels want to do at this point in the story is sing praise to God, which itself is a revelatory act.

The angelic hymn ascribes glory to God, as a good hymn should. It also declares "peace" to the world. Peace was a word you might expect to hear in a first-century gospel about the Roman emperor or his officials. A lot of Roman propaganda boasted about the peace Rome brought to people within the empire's borders. It also referred to the first emperor, Augustus, as a savior. The angels of Luke imply that God's peace has a whole different quality, ushered in by a very different Savior. You can detect a hint of protest as you hear the angels sing. The empire is hardly what it's cracked up to be.

Once, after a Christmas Eve service a few years ago, my mother said something to me along the lines of, "What did you do to the Christmas story?" I pressed her for more information and learned she didn't like the translation of the second half of the angel's song as it was read in the service: "On earth peace among those whom he [God] favors!" She preferred the old King James Version: "On earth peace, good will toward men." I had to reassure her that I had nothing to do with the change. There's no cabal of Bible scholars holding meetings to find ways to ruin people's favorite Bible verses.

Her complaint wasn't about ditching the archaic word *men* to translate the Greek word for "people." She thought that the newer translation limits the scope of who gets to experience peace. Shouldn't peace and good will go to all people? She has a point, but I told her

95

that we don't get to decide how to translate based on our preferences about how God should operate. I think she was unconvinced. The Greek syntax in Luke 2:14 is famously ambiguous (well, famous to nerds like me and my professional colleagues). The matter is also complicated by the fact that surviving Greek manuscripts don't agree. A medieval copyist's addition or subtraction of a single letter in Greek has made a big difference. In any case, at the end of the day the angels sing a prayer for peace, even if the specifics remain a little vague to us. So I choose to focus on that—the value of peace—as opposed to trying to prevail in a disagreement with my mother.

Back in the fields, the shepherds witness and hear things that probably strike them as unbelievable. They must therefore understand that what's happening is a big deal. But what is happening? What exactly is the gospel—the "good news of great joy" at this moment?

Luke provides at least two answers to that question. The first one requires us to consider what expectations the shepherds might associate with the promise of the Messiah (the Anointed One). Not all Jews in the first century were hoping for someone called the Messiah to emerge, but those who were had a range of expectations. There was no single expected job description for the Messiah. It would depend on which documents or teachers you were consulting. At the same time, the general expectation was that God would designate, send, or raise up a deliverer. That image of being anointed means to be appointed and commissioned for a special purpose. The Old Testament describes ceremonies in which kings, priests, and prophets are anointed with oil as a sign of their responsibilities to work on God's behalf.

A number of expectations connected to the Messiah's arrival involve ushering in a new era of righteousness, peace, and security. Sometimes that entails getting rid of enemies or agents of wickedness.

In many expectations, the promise of resurrection of the dead and a glorious postmortem existence is associated with the Messiah's appearance. So maybe "Hark! The Herald Angels Sing" isn't simply projecting; maybe the hymn really is able to unpack the weight of significance that comes with merely identifying Jesus as the Messiah or the Christ (remember, those two terms are synonyms).

The Gospels, particularly Matthew and Luke, lift up the importance of the Messiah's connection to King David. If you read David's story in 1–2 Samuel you'll probably come away from it thinking he looks more like Tony Soprano than a king whom you'd want your children grow up to revere, yet David was remembered as Israel's greatest king. He represented to many an era when people most felt most secure and when God's protection of the nation was evident, despite David's obvious faults.

In addition, these are *shepherds* who hear the angels sing. What was David's role in his family as a young boy? He watched the sheep (1 Samuel 16:11). Where did David live? The little town of Bethlehem (1 Samuel 16:1). What did the prophet Samuel do to David there? He anointed him as Israel's next king (1 Samuel 16:13). In the time of ancient Israel, a common metaphor for a king who ruled on God's behalf was a shepherd (see, for example, Jeremiah 23:1-4). The angels' appearance to shepherds, of all people, is hardly random.

Sometimes I hear sermons that describe ancient shepherds as people with bad reputations, as if the wider population thought that shepherds were all cheats, liars, and crooks (pun intended). There's no basis for such a claim. No evidence for such stereotypes exists. These aren't ancient society's worst people being invited to the manger. Nor are they exactly powerful people. They are reminders of kingship and the promise of a better future being born in Bethlehem. They are ordinary folks encouraged to witness an extraordinary infant. Remember Mary's song, which we explored in chapter 3. God is upending the ways in which a society orders honor and privilege.

The second reason why Jesus's birth constitutes "good news" is accessible to us readers much more than it is to the shepherds in the narrative. We are allowed to eavesdrop on all the action that came before this passage, especially during the Annunciation, the Visitation, the Magnificat, and the Benedictus. We have insight into Jesus's origins and know he's not just another David; he's no ordinary human king. I discussed the Incarnation briefly in chapter 3. Does God send an anointed human agent to do God's bidding, or does God come to do the work? Somehow, both. God is present. God is among us. Christmas is, after all, an epiphany. Yet the angelic host doesn't leave the fields and pay a visit to the place where Jesus lies. His mother and father can watch over this epiphany for now. Mary will ponder everything. It's all so ordinary, from one point of view. Anyone who lives nearby would not hear anything unusual in the baby's cries. God arrives as a fragile body, surrounded by high hopes.

Other voices will soon speak, allowing us to unpack what that means.

Those other voices belong to two wise, experienced people. While it appears that Jesus's birth catches the attention of only a collection of angel-guided shepherds, when Mary and Joseph subsequently bring their infant to the Temple, as Jewish law instructs them, others notice. Simeon and Anna recognize Jesus for who he is and reveal his significance to anyone who will listen.

Although Simeon and Anna appear nowhere else in the Bible, Luke tells us much about them, at least in comparison to the shepherds. Their piety gets significant attention. The narrative explicitly identifies

Anna as a prophet, while Simeon's insights from the Holy Spirit imply that we should consider him as a prophet as well.

Simeon's experience cuts in two ways, for he gets to meet the Messiah while also realizing that probably the only thing standing between him and death has now evaporated. Maybe you had an ailing relative who was able to hang on long enough to make it through one more Christmas, to attend a family wedding, or to witness the birth of a grandchild before succumbing to death. Simeon evokes that kind of holy—and fortunate—bittersweetness.

In the form of a public prayer to God, Simeon offers the third canticle we find in Luke 1–2. Like the other two, its traditional name (the Nunc dimittis) comes from the beginning of the song's translation into Latin. The words of his lyrical prayer reveal things to Mary and Joseph and also to Luke's audience. Jesus himself is the embodiment of salvation. Moreover, this Messiah will be good news for others in addition to the people of Israel, meaning Jews. He is also "a light for revelation to the gentiles" (2:32). That simple phrase evokes a range of scriptural memories, stretching back to God's promise to Abraham. The Greek word translated "gentiles" literally means "nations," so one detects echoes of God's pledge to bless all the nations (or peoples) of the earth through Abraham's lineage (Genesis 18:18). Simeon's language also recalls passages in the Book of Isaiah that look forward to a time when Gentiles will glimpse and respond to the radiance of God's salvation shining forth (for example, Isaiah 42:6; 52:10; 60:1-3).

We cannot overstate the scope of what Simeon announces. There is more to it than "God is keeping an old promise." Rather, in the arrival of Jesus Christ, God is keeping *the* big promise, the one in which God blesses the whole world through God's faithfulness to

Abraham's offspring. Notice that Simeon does not imply that God intends to bypass or ignore Jews in the process. In no way does he prophesy about Gentiles *replacing* Jews as the apple of God's eye. The thrust of Simeon's claim is all about expansion, inclusion, and belonging. He's announcing that we're going to need a lot more chairs at the table.

Anna seconds the motion when she erupts with praise and shares good news with "all who were looking for the redemption of Jerusalem." She could, like Simeon, have ancient promises on the mind, given that the exuberance of Isaiah 52:8-10 resonates with the hope she shares, as Luke summarizes it. Jerusalem is not just a place in Luke—and in its sequel, the book of Acts—it's also a symbol. It represents captivity and waywardness in some passages, but it also has a centripetal force to it as the place where people gather and reside as a community brought together by the Holy Spirit to share God's welcome with one another. That's a big part of what it means for the city to experience "redemption."

All of this sounds amazing, but it has to be qualified by words Simeon speaks privately to Mary in verses 34-35. If anyone's expecting the way forward to consist of the Christ taking an effortless victory lap, they should reconsider. Jesus will be the cause of falling and rising, activities that Mary sang about back in Luke 1:52. Jesus will suffer opposition, in the process exposing people's resistance to God and the salvation God provides. And, most chilling of all, "A sword will pierce your [Mary's] own soul, too." What a thing to say to a new mother about the road ahead of her as a parent. I mean, no sane first-time parents leave the hospital's neonatal unit saying to themselves, "This is going to be so easy!" But we who know the rest of Luke's story understand that Simeon is correct. Realism crashes into the elation.

That crash reminds us that Advent and then Christmas mark beginnings, not culminations. They launch Jesus into the world. We follow. When Simeon's and Anna's voices subside, the revelation of Christmas reaches its end in Luke. What's next? To borrow a line from Howard Thurman's simple yet moving poem about turning from Christmas adoration to year-round action:

The work of Christmas begins[3]

The work of Christmas consists of tangible deeds of compassion and mercy. Christmas lays a commission on Jesus. And on us.

IN CONCLUSION

Angels and prophets speak through dreams, declarations, songs, conversations, and warnings. Their voices reveal things about Jesus and what he will do, even before he knows how to sit up on his own. These revelations nudge us to keep reading, for that is the only way to make more sense of them. We have to observe what all of these promises look like in action and where they lead. Presumably God could transform the world all at once by speaking a new one into being, with societies remade to preserve peace, love, and justice for all. Instead, God chooses a much more hands-on approach, a lived approach.

This book and our shared exploration of Advent end with the arrival of Christmas, so other guides will have to accompany you into the rest of the stories told in the Gospels. I think the revelations we've explored in this chapter will hold up well as you read on. That's why it's beneficial to revisit these scriptural revelations every Advent and Christmas. We can view them in retrospect and then recalibrate our longings and our efforts accordingly, from year to year.

Angels and prophets bear witness to God's reliability. We like it when others keep their promises to us, the good promises at least. The angelic and prophetic promises are big ones though. Christmas opens the door of a vault containing God's ultimate intentions for the entire world and the well-being of all.

When preachers deliver sermons about that on Christmas Eve, I imagine many in the congregation are saying in their heads, "Ha! Prove it." These promises don't lend themselves to easy proof, though. How does a person prove it to you when they say, "I love you"? Precious gifts and kind gestures aren't a bad way to start, of course. But that person needs to walk with you over time, through ups and downs. We gradually accumulate signs—indicators—of love. The preacher— or you or I—can offer only assorted signs of God's commitment to humanity and to the skeptic in the pew. Those signs of God's presence may look rather low-key and ordinary: caring community, changed lives, a demonstrated resolve to doing justice, kindness to a stranger, mercy to someone who was dealt a bad hand or who made a mistake. The signs in the Christmas story aren't necessarily earth-shattering either: the name the angel speaks to Joseph in a dream and the bands of cloth and the manger that the angel tells the shepherds to seek. Those are signs that don't blare a message with unmistakable clarity. They are signs that become more vivid to those who are curious and who are willing to take the next step in trust.

Angels and prophets also reveal the arrival of salvation. "Save" is a churchy word, too often thrown around as if we should envision a net trying to pluck unsuspecting people out of quicksand. But the biblical words behind the idea of salvation refer to healing, rescuing, preserving, and making people whole. I hear invitations in those words, not a hunting expedition.

Everything about the arrival of Jesus is salvation. Christmas is the onset of salvation and deliverance. Salvation isn't reserved for the cross. It encapsulates everything about who Jesus is and what he does. Salvation is an event, a happening, a person. Salvation occurs wherever Jesus is, whether you go to him or he comes to you. Let us adore him.

AFTERWORD

Life after Advent

Who is this Messiah we expect to arrive at the end of Advent? How will he help us better understand ourselves and our lives?

For a long time, artists have been interested in depicting the infant Jesus with his mother, especially in conformity to a classical Madonna and Child motif. You've probably seen examples of paintings in which Mary holds her baby, giving viewers a good look at both of their facial expressions.

Some of those paintings from the Middle Ages are good for comic relief, because they make Jesus look like a middle-aged man in a tiny body. Search online for images of the Crevole Madonna by Duccio di Buoninsegna if you don't believe me. That's just one instance among many. Jesus's body is the size of a small child's, but his proportions and shape resemble a miniature adult's. His head almost looks like it was photoshopped.

Medieval artists who followed those conventions for a period of history were trying to express a mystery: that the Son of God can't be confined to a single point in time. Even as an infant, Jesus carries within him the knowledge and wisdom that would help him change the world. In some of those paintings, therefore, the child holds a scroll or a book, even though every actual baby I've ever encountered would try to eat the paper as opposed to reading it.

I appreciate the intention of the artistic style, for it urges us at Christmas to approach the manger to meet a Savior who transcends time. If all of salvation is wrapped up in him, in Jesus himself, then we should glimpse his birth, his ministry, his death, his resurrection, and his glorification all at once. In a way, Jesus is constantly arriving for us, and he has constantly already arrived. If Jesus is "the power of God and the wisdom of God" (1 Corinthians 1:24)—not just that he *possesses* all of that, but if he *is* all of that—then we need reminders that he somehow contains all power and wisdom within himself. The Holy Infant, so tender and mild at Christmas, will grow up and call out the oppressions that threaten the world. He will have the vision and the voice to discern, promise, and embody a different reality—a new reality.

With all respect to classical artists, however, I also find that it's easier, at least for me, to ponder those mysteries about the fullness of Christ without having to look at a painting that makes me think of Danny DeVito sitting on Mary's lap.

The artistic practice of placing an adult head on an infant carries with it a significant risk, which deserves our attention in a book like this. If there is a reluctance to portray Jesus as an infant in every way, does that mean there's discomfort about making him look too much like us? Is there something about a dewy-eyed and vulnerable baby's face that portrays a Christ who is too human for some Christians' comfort?

There shouldn't be. In the only story the Gospels tell about Jesus between his infancy and his arrival in the wilderness to be baptized by John, he is twelve years old (Luke 2:41-52). He ditches his family and goes to the Jerusalem temple to have conversations with religious leaders. After his parents recover him, in the last line of the scene we read: "And Jesus increased in wisdom and in years and in divine and human favor." He grows and matures, like any child should. Yes, the Bible tells us that in Jesus "the whole fullness of deity dwells bodily" (Colossians 2:9), yet our Scriptures also imply that, to quote one of my favorite Christmas hymns, "day by day like us he grew."[1] In Jesus, those two assertions are not contradictions.

My point is that Jesus, although extraordinary, also comes to us as one of us. Remember John 1:14, which we explored in chapter 3: "The Word became flesh and lived among us." God becomes known to us most clearly, most viscerally, and most intimately as one of us. The church makes that audacious claim to the world every Christmas. The child—an actual child—is Emmanuel (Matthew 1:23).

God's choice to become known to us in this way tells us a lot about God and about God's desire to enter into close relationship with humanity. It's a desire fueled by God's love for the world, the Bible insists (see John 3:16). Loving the world isn't a Pollyannaish adventure for God, for the world is difficult terrain. In particular, in the crucifixion of Jesus—in the violence done to his body—we witness God's commitment to entering into solidarity with the people in this world who suffer the greatest dehumanization and dishonor.

The embodiment of God also tells us a lot about ourselves and about the reasons why God expects us to treat one another well and with such honor.

As an embodied human being, Jesus Christ grows, learns, struggles, loves, celebrates, prays, criticizes, weeps, receives kindness, helps others, suffers, bleeds, dies, and enters into new life. In doing so, God honors the capacity of human bodies and the potential of human life. In other words, through his life Jesus demonstrates that bodies matter and are the means by which we encounter God. If we want to commune with God, we don't need to climb a mountain, sit in a dark room for hours, or somehow disconnect our souls from our bodies to reach some higher plane of existence. Our bodies are the places, the locations, where God meets us and blesses us. In our bodies we learn what it is like to be loved, to be comforted in our grief, to be celebrated, to be forgiven, to be seen, and to be treated with dignity. We learn all of that from other people if we are fortunate; we learn it from God if we open ourselves up.

Jesus's followers have a regrettable legacy, however, of occasionally telling people that their bodies are sources of distraction, ignorance, or evil. Some preachers and teachers have taught people not to trust their feelings, not to heed their desires, not to embrace their identity, not to enjoy life, and not to love themselves. Even more, some Christians have neglected the suffering of other people's bodies because they have been taught that all they need to worry about is saving souls for a future existence.

As I remind my students, sometimes we have to un-teach certain teachings that have led the church to err in the past. Making meaningful corrections and thereby giving voice to the gospel with integrity requires persistent action, not just words.

To join ourselves with Christ is to commit ourselves to uphold the dignity of what it means to be human—for all humanity. The more that human dignity and basic human rights are under assault in this world, the more urgent is the need for our commitment. As we learned in chapter 1, while we explored those challenging apocalyptic messages that Jesus teaches soon before his arrest, the church has a calling to live out, all the more so when things are at their worst. Joining ourselves with Christ is to anticipate opportunities to stumble on the goodness and presence of God in our dealings with other people. It involves rejecting attitudes and policies that dehumanize both individuals and groups. It entails countering cruelty with unremitting kindness. It is to pledge ourselves to generosity and mercy in our personal interactions with others and in the more expansive laws and practices that affect the lives of real people, because in Jesus we learn to "regard no one from a human point of view" (2 Corinthians 5:16).

That means we expect to encounter Christ himself in each person around us—in every body.

I've spoken throughout this book of our longings and our hope. What do we mean when we say we long for God to set the world to rights? For me, I long for a world that enacts what I've just described. What do we mean when we say that Advent gives us the power to embrace hope—a confident and therefore active hope, in which we are so confident of what's coming that we eagerly play our part? For me, that comes down to Jesus and the full stories that the Gospels tell about him. He shows the way.

And he promises to arrive among us over and over.

Advent provides us an opportunity to open our imaginations and to ponder mysteries about the past, present, and future. The voices of Advent are voices of invitation, beckoning us to come closer and to risk a little more. They are voices that acknowledge and share our longings. The voices call to us, urging us not to stand by, but to follow where Jesus goes, as he leads the way into life after Advent.

NOTES

Introduction

1 Phillips Brooks, lyrics (1868), "O Little Town of Bethlehem," *Glory to God: The Presbyterian Hymnal* (Louisville: Westminster John Knox, 2013), #121.

2 Justin Martyr, First Apology, in *St. Justin Martyr: The First and Second Apologies*, ed. Leslie William Barnard (Mahwah, NJ: Paulist, 1997), 52.3.

3 Paul Gerhardt, lyrics (1653), "O Lord, How Shall I Meet You," trans. Catherine Winkworth et al. (1863), *Glory to God: The Presbyterian Hymnal*, #104.

4 "The Coming of Jesus in Our Midst"; reprinted in *The Living Pulpit* 6, no. 4 (October–December 1997), 39.

Chapter 1

1 Bach weaves additional scriptural themes and phrases into the piece, contributing to its peaceful and hopeful interpretation of Christ's return. For example, he turns to the Bible's erotic poetry (Song of Solomon 2:16-17; 6:3) to characterize Jesus as our beloved or friend, and the fourth movement offers echoes of a soaring promise of salvation (Isaiah 52:7-10).

2 It is difficult to summarize all the ancient literature—apocalypses and other writings that include the same sorts of themes—because there's not a single way to capture the range of what we find in the relevant writings. In this paragraph I've drawn on a short, general summary from a book that is quite accessible if you are interested in learning more about these ancient writings and their influence on the New Testament: Greg Carey, *Apocalyptic Literature in the New Testament* (Nashville: Abingdon, 2016), 14-16.

3 Part of Luke's version of the speech offers a description of Jerusalem under siege (Luke 21:20-24) that corresponds well to other surviving ancient testimony about the Romans' assault on the city. Luke's original audience would have known that the city's "desolation" mentioned in those verses applies to the Temple as well. Also, vague statements in Matthew 24:15 and Mark 13:14 probably refer to a Roman commander's desecration of the Temple just before he had his soldiers demolish it. In other words, the

Notes

Gospels are obviously making associations between Jesus's speech and events that occurred close to the time that the Gospels were composed.

Chapter 2

1 The relevant passage is in book 18 of *Antiquities*, §116-219.

2 The Gospels associate John with Elijah, but not all of them make the same connections. In Matthew, Jesus suggests John is a kind of reappearance of Elijah, but that could mean a variety of things (Matthew 11:14; 17:11-13). In other places the relationship is left more ambiguous (Mark 9:13), or John flatly denies that he is Elijah (John 1:21). Apparently there was disagreement in the early church about how to describe John and his relevance for situating Jesus within the larger context of God's promises and their fulfillment.

3 Bryan Stevenson, *Just Mercy: A Story of Justice and Redemption* (New York: Random House, 2014).

4 Charles Wesley, lyrics (1744), "Come, Thou Long-Expected Jesus," *Glory to God: The Presbyterian Hymnal*, #82 and #83.

5 William Chatterton Dix, lyrics (1871), "What Child Is This," *Glory to God: The Presbyterian Hymnal*, #145.

Chapter 3

1 Ken Bible, lyrics (1996), "Love Has Come," *Glory to God: The Presbyterian Hymnal*, #110.

2 Jan Richardson, "Gabriel's Annunciation," reprinted at "Journey with Jesus," https://www.journeywithjesus.net/poemsandprayers/2432-gabriel-s-annunciation.

3 Pre-9th-century Latin prose; Trans. composite, "O Come, O Come, Emmanuel," *Glory to God: The Presbyterian Hymnal*, #88.

4 John Francis Wade, lyrics (c. 1743), "O Come, All Ye Faithful," trans. Frederick Oakeley, *Glory to God: The Presbyterian Hymnal*, #133.

Chapter 4

1 Amy-Jill Levine offers a brief summary of that history in *Light of the World: A Beginner's Guide to Advent* (Nashville: Abingdon, 2019), 123-125. For a discussion that takes more of an intermediate-level approach in terms of its amount of detail and technicality, see Amy-Jill Levine and Marc Zvi Brettler, *The Bible With and Without Jesus: How Jews and Christians Read the Same Stories Differently* (New York: HarperOne, 2020), 255-283.

2   Charles Wesley, lyrics (1739), "Hark! The Herald Angels Sing," *Glory to God: The Presbyterian Hymnal*, #119.

3   "The Work of Christmas," in *The Mood of Christmas* (Richmond, IN: Friends United, 1973), 23.

Afterword

1   Cecil Frances Alexander, lyrics (1848), "Once in Royal David's City," *Glory to God: The Presbyterian Hymnal*, #140.

Watch videos based on *Voices of Advent* with Matthew L. Skinner through Amplify Media.

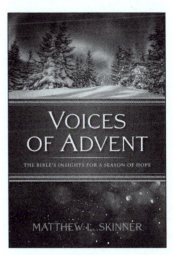

Amplify Media is a multimedia platform that delivers high-quality, searchable content with an emphasis on Wesleyan perspectives for churchwide, group, or individual use on any device at any time. In a world of sometimes overwhelming choices, Amplify gives church leaders and congregants media capabilities that are contemporary, relevant, effective and, most important, affordable and sustainable.

With *Amplify Media* church leaders can:

- Provide a reliable source of Christian content through a Wesleyan lens for teaching, training, and inspiration in a customizable library
- Deliver their own preaching and worship content in a way the congregation knows and appreciates
- Build the church's capacity to innovate with engaging content and accessible technology
- Equip the congregation to better understand the Bible and its application
- Deepen discipleship beyond the church walls

Ask your group leader or pastor about Amplify Media and sign up today at www.AmplifyMedia.com.